THE GAEAN REACH GAZETTEER

A SUPPLEMENT FOR THE GAEAN REACH ROLEPLAYING GAME

BASED ON THE CLASSIC SCIENCE FICTION OF JACK VANCE

BY PETER FREEMAN & JIM WEBSTER

CREDITS

PUBLISHER: Simon Rogers

AUTHORS: Peter Freeman, Jim Webster

LAYOUT: Chris Huth

ART DIRECTION: Chris Huth

COVER ART: Chris Huth

INTERIOR ART: Chris Huth

COPYEDITING: Christopher Smith Adair

CONTENTS

GAZETTEER

For your edification and delight I have toiled unceasingly. Only a person of the highest calibre could have hardened his heart as I have and unblushingly allowed so many deadlines to drift past.

Deadlines, editors, pah! Nailing them upside down to a church door is too good for suchlike. But still, I have laboured. I have worn out a mouse (plus two sommeliers and a wandering flagellant); I have peered at maps, faded and stained by the passing of the decades; I have squinted under strange lights and discoursed with people whose skin has been tanned by fiercer suns.

And I have made a pile of all I have found.

Some may call me capricious. Indeed the word whimsical has even been used. Beware of any who use such words; they tend to sip small beer from small glasses and pay poorly, pushing thin piles of scrip across the table, when a true aficionado would shower you with hard currency, suitcases full of it, used notes, non-sequential, in refreshingly large denominations.

There, I have spoken. Read on, but at your peril, lest you glimpse a universe so rich that mere reality seems bland and inconsequential.

— Jarim Oebs, Associate Interlocutor of Galaxeology [de-tenured], Dagglesby University, Cicely

Abbreviations

AS = *Araminta Station*, New English Library, 1989
BD = *The Book of Dreams*, Coronet Books, 1982
EOE = *Ecce and Old Earth*, New English Library, 1991
F = *The Face*, Coronet Books, 1981
GE = *Galactic Effectuator*, Coronet Books, 1983
GP = *The Gray Prince*, Coronet Books, 1976
KM = *The Killing Machine*, Coronet Books, 1980
L = *Lurulu*, Voyager, 2006
MA= *Marune: Alastor 933*, DAW Books, 1975
MT = *Maske: Thaery*, Fontana, 1978
NL = *Night Lamp*, Voyager, 1996
PL = *The Palace of Love*, Coronet Books, 1980
PoC = *Ports of Call*, Voyager, 1999
SK = *The Star King*, Mayflower, 1973
T = *Throy*, New English Library, 1993
TA= *Trullion Alastor 2262*, Grafton, 1987
WA = *Wyst: Alastor 1716*, Coronet Books, 1980

ACHERNAR
KM 112 | PoC 91

This world is the home of the Achernar Central School of Forensic Linguistics.

ADAR MOUNTAINS
BD 19

On the world of **Copus**, these mountains are a source of Mersilin rugs.

AGAVE
T 141

I have been reliably informed that "the Bestiary is under the ruins of Agave"; what the Bestiary is, or where Agave is, these are matters on which I, for one, can shine no light whatsoever.

AGLABAT
KM 113

On the planet of **Thamber**, in **Misk**, it was originally a fishing village; it is now a city behind a wall of dark brown stone.

AIRY GULCH
BD 94

A huge gulch deep in the **Skak Range** on **Boniface**.

ALASTOR CLUSTER
GE 78 | MA 7

Even in distant parts of the Gaean Reach, Alastor Cluster is known as the home of the starmenters. In reality it is far more civilised that that. It is a node of thirty thousand live stars plus unnumbered dead ones on the inner rim of the galaxy. It has the Unfortunate Waste before, the Nonestic Gulf beyond, and the Gaean Reach a sparkling haze to the side. It is ruled by the Connatic from his palace on the world **Numenes**, and order is maintained by the Whelm, his space navy.

Still, it has to be said that the Whelm is not maintained purely to provide steady careers for the deserving younger sons of minor landowners. Starmenters are far more of a problem in Alastor Cluster than they are elsewhere in Gaean space. Save perhaps for the **Primarchic**, and it is from the Primarchic that a proportion of the Alastor Cluster starmenters seem to come.

ALCYDON
PoC 167 | L 198

To visit the modestly renown Pan-Arts Museum (one of the few things this world is known for), land at the **Duvray** spaceport. For relaxation afterwards, the editorial staff recommends Coiry Beach.

ALCYONE
BD 48

This world is the home of the Pallas Technical Institute, which is still (in spite of rumours to the contrary) located at **Pallas**.

ALGENIB IX
BD 48

Known only as the world of origin of A. Gieselman, a murder victim, who at the time dwelt at **Long Parade**, in the town of **Espandencia**.

ALOYSIUS
SK 51 | PL 27 | F 5

Also known as Vega VI, a planet of the **Rigel Concourse**, it is the sister planet to **Boniface** and **Cuthbert**. One of the first planets settled, it shows signs of considerable human antiquity, especially as some of the original settlers refused to build anything that wasn't in keeping with the environment, and their influence remains even when they are long gone. The seasonal fluctuations are severe, winters cold, summers hot, due to the axis being inclined at 31.7 degrees (in comparison **Earth**'s axis is inclined at just over 7 degrees). There are nine continents; Dorgan (otherwise known as Marcy's Land) is the largest, **New Wexford** its chief city. Due to a long history of low taxes and favourable regulation, it is an important commercial centre. The smallest of the continents is Gavin's Land, on which the city of **Pontefract** is situated. Two others of interest are Bodart's Land and Dimpey's Land.

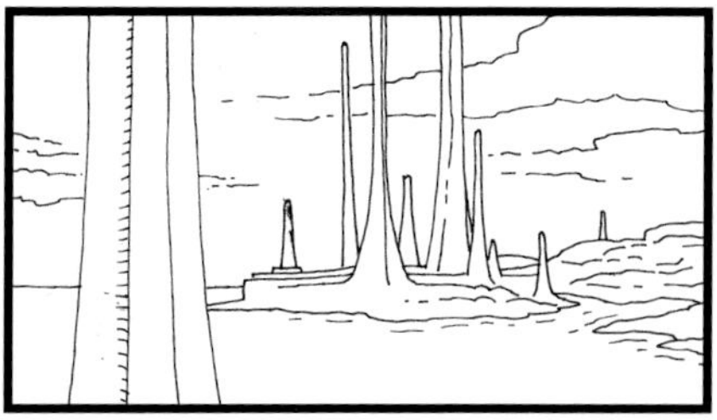

ALPHANOR
SK 32 | F 195 | AS 13

The capital planet of the **Rigel Concourse** circles Rigel. There are seven continents and innumerable islands, but three quarters of the surface is ocean. Autochthonous life is vigorous, the human inhabitants mainly fair, brown haired and of medium height. The continents, **Phrygia**, **Umbria**, **Lusitania**, **Scythia**, **Etruria**, **Lydia** and **Lycia**, are all of similar size, and from space it has been remarked they look like seven petals of a flower. Each continent is divided into provinces which are again divided into prefectures, districts and wards; the latter are population blocks of five thousand persons. Each ward committee sends a representative to the prefectural diet which sends one to the provincial congress, which then sends one to the continental parliament. Each parliament elects seven rectors to the Grand Council at **Avente** in the Sea Province of Umbria.

Architecturally the planet is known for glass towers that are regarded as pretentious by those who visit from off-world, but are assumed to be a sign of a mature architecture by the inhabitants.

On Alphanor are produced the beers Vergence and True Companion; it exports furniture and panels of semi-precious stone.

ALPHARD THE LONELY
KM 30

One of the stars of the **Rigel Concourse**, it is the sun of the world **Quinine**.

ALPHECCA NINE
AS 17

This is the world on which Sarsenopolis is situated. The main religion of the population is the Quadriplar Revelation.

ALPHERATZ
BD 137 | GE 155

It is the world on which the Great Tri-Ocean Canal is situated. I suppose it is not too much to expect that the world has three oceans?

ALSACE
F 174

A region on **Earth**; Alsatian vinegar is still exported to far worlds.

AMBEULES
PL 38, 69

A suburb of **Rolingshaven** on the west coast of Europe, **Earth**. It is on the river **Gaas**. For the tourist we would suggest the following places of evening entertainment: Mikmak's Cabaret, Paru's, Der Fliegende Hollander, the Blue

Pearl, the Sunset Café on the Boulevard Castel Vivence, Zadiel's All-World Rendezvous and the Celestial Harmony Café. It is unwise to attempt to visit all of them in the same evening.

AMSTERDAM PL 47

A city in Europe on **Earth**.

ANDELMORE F 176

The house of the Floristys in the suburb of **Llalarkno** on **Methel**.

ANDROMEDA 6011 IV AS 282 | EOE 25

A junction world where passengers from **Mircea's Wisp** transfer to ships heading for **Earth**. There are two cities mentioned, Watertown and Port Blue Lamp.

ANTHONY PRINGLE'S WORLD EOE 258

Nothing is known of this world other than the fact that the starport is at Mersey.

AQUARIUS SECTOR PL 108

One of the great constellation/sectors into which the universe is divided.

ARAMINTA STATION AS 12

Situated on the world of **Cadwal**, it is an enclave of approximately one hundred square miles on the east coast of the continent of **Deucas**. This is where the Naturalist Society of Earth established an administrative agency to enforce the terms of the charter under which Cadwal is governed. There are the six great houses (both lineages and buildings): Wook House, Clattuc House, Veder House, Diffin House, Laverty House, and Offaw House, all founded by the original superintendents, and each inhabited by the extended families. A mile south on the **Leur River** and the edge of the settlement lives the Conservator, the head superintendent, in Riverview House. There is also a hotel, an airport (with Yip dormitories), a hospital, schools, a theatre (the Orpheum) and vineyards, and it is from Araminta Station that one has access to a dozen wilderness lodges. The Bolo Hills are part of the station area. The Beach Road runs from the dock where the ferry runs to **Lutwen Atoll** and parallels the beach running past the lyceum (or upper school) to Riverview House and meets with Wansey Way at the lyceum. Clattuc House is on Wansey Way, which leads past the lyceum to the Mummers' warehouse where theatrical costumes are stored; the **River Wann** is parallel to Wansey Way. Old Arbour is a popular bar off Wansey Way.

South of the airport are plantations and vineyards, then the River Wann (which meets the sea at the Wann River bar) and the Big Lagoon, which marks the edge of the enclave. Then, heading south from the enclave proper, you see a placid savannah, with hills to the west that become the Muldoon Mountains, through which comes Flutterby Pass, which funnels migrating butterflies down the Maroli Valley to the sea. At the foot is Maroli Meadow, where migrating butterflies nip of their wings and run for the sea. Also close by, near enough to be considered a slight potential threat, are the Maughrim Mountains. These are higher, wilder and further away than the Muldoon Mountains but are home of the night-flying gambril; the larger ones can carry a person and could certainly carry off a small child.

The Joint Winery is half a mile from the airport, blending second-grade wines for each of the six house wineries.

A considerable distance from the enclave, but administered by and considered part of it, the Cape Journal Roadway is a penal road at the far south of Deucas. It is a road-building project where felons break rocks between Crazy Katy Lake and Mile-high Falls.

ARBELLO GE 45

Wolden Port is the spaceport. Indeed it is noticeable that there are a number of worlds about which all we know is the name of the spaceport. This is, I suppose, something to be lamented, but, frankly, on the current budget there isn't much we can do about it.

Anyone who is travelling in the vicinity of any of these little known worlds who is good enough to send the publisher information gleaned by personal experience will find the publishers not ungrateful. Ungenerous, yes, but never ungrateful.

ARBONETTA GE 78

A world about which we know nothing save that men wear their hair in varnished ringlets.

ARCHIMBAL L 177

A planet on the space lanes near **Avente**; the spaceport is Organon. The population is known for its ability to work best in communal groups. A note to concerned travellers: neither beer nor ale can be purchased in Organon.

ARCTURUS IV BD 9

The fourth planet circling the star Arcturus. **Bugtown** is one of the towns there.

ARCTURUS LEGEND PoC 155

Frankly, we know nothing; it may be an illusion, a figment of humanity's collective imagination, a destination of desire? Should you discover the truth of this place, and, provided it is not too sordid, the editors would doubtless be gratified to learn more. But note all researches must be at the researcher's own expense.

ARD COURT KM 22

The broad area where **Ard Street** opens out somewhat as it reaches the sea wall. The court is full of the smell of Sandusker cooking and the area does attract any Sanduskers who come to **Alphanor**.

ARD HOOK SK 89

A bay with a line of bluffs on the shores of the ocean at **Avente**.

ARD STREET KM 22

A street in **Sailmaker Beach** on **Alphanor**.

ARGO NAVIS L 41

A region of space.

ARGO NAVIS 961 F 21

A star, also known as **Cora**; the desert world of **Dar Sai** is its third planet.

ARMONGOL BD 102

The home of the "Natural Jungle League." I realise this is indecisive. Is Armongol a world? A town? A house with a singularly pretentious name? Frankly, I don't know but suspect the foremost.

ARRABUS WA 11, 53

Arrabus is considered the powerhouse of **Wyst**; the inhabitants work two brief periods of "drudge" a week plus another two hours of "maintenance" at the block where they reside. After that their time is their own. The only food is "gruff" and "deedle," with the occasional dish of "wobbly"; there is nothing else. Gruff is a cake; deedle is a viscous white liquid. "Bonter," or natural food, is almost unknown, given distribution problems of getting it to three billion people who steadfastly refuse to work. The locals will brew their own alcohol from leftover food, but there is no official brewery.

There are conventional farms along the edge of the hills that line the littoral. **Pamatra Valley** is a rich agricultural area.

The spaceport is to the east of the Uncibal River.

Disjerferact is the carnival strip along the mudflats by the sea.

The nature of the Arrabin is perhaps captured by the view from the prospect deck on the Uncibal River, where you see the oncoming sea of faces, each merging into the next, numberless and uncountable.

ASPIDISKE IV EOE 258

This world is situated at the head of the **Argo Navis** sector; the starport is **Star Home**.

ASTROPOLIS
PL 151

A city, a planet? In all candour I don't know. The inhabitants have thirteen gods and make them compete for high god-hood.

ATAR
PL 108

A city at the south of the hourglass continent on the planet of **Sogdian**, circling the star, **Miel**.

ATHMORE VIOLET
BD 88

A ridge in the **Skak Range** on **Boniface**. A local, Bugardoig, mines the ridge for alexandrites.

AVENTE
SK 57

A city in the Sea Province of **Umbria** on **Alphanor**.

AVENTE
L 177

A world not far from **Blenkinsop** and Falziel, the spaceport is Chancelade; the people are tolerant, but intensely aware of their own individuality. Note that when Avente is mentioned, it is wise to assume that the city on **Alphanor** is being discussed.

AXELBARREN
NL 93, 95

At the city of Glist on Axelbarren, there is the Aeolian Academy. A very fine school but very expensive, it overlooks the Greater Kanjieir Sea, and, at least some of the time, the girls are reputed to camp and take lessons on the beach. Cloud Island may be in the same sea; it is a place of beauty for summer houses by the beach.

AXISTIL
GE 11

Axistil is on the planet **Maz**; the centre of the town is under Triarchic jurisdiction. The Gaean sector includes the Gaean spaceport and the suburb of Dogtown. Far Dogtown, in the native Gomaz territory, is beyond Gaean authority and is a refuge for criminals. The Liss and the Olefract both have their own sectors and spaceports. The best human hotel is the Beyranion overlooking the plaza. The Avenue of Lost Souls runs from the central plaza through Dogtown and peters out in Far Dogtown. For those staying in Dogtown, the Last Resort is a reasonable hotel; Far Dogtown does not have any reasonable hotels. In the northwest corner of the plaza is the Maz Transport depot; they run carriers out from Axistil to the various Gomaz castles and lodges. Anyone can ride freely on the carriers, but only Gomaz can disembark at the castle stations.

AZULIAS
MA 34

A world in the **Alphanor** cluster where the population rarely have blood type RC3.

BAGSHILLY PLAIN
F 66

A region on **Dar Sai** near **Gaggar's Shade**.

BALLYHOLT WOODS
BD 13

A prosperous neighbourhood to the north of **Pontefract** full of splendid mansions and the fine houses of the more than usually prosperous.

BALMATH
TA 180

A world where the inhabitants, at least when off planet, wear a jade locket. It is probably in the **Alastor Cluster**.

BALTIMORE
KM 120

A city on **Earth**. It is the home of the magazine *Galactic Quarterly*.

BANACRE
GE 32

This place provides a good market for angelfish. Frankly I don't know whether it is a world or a small town, or something in-between. Frankly, I suspect the former is more plausible. After all there is only so much angelfish that even the most prestigious small-town fish emporium can sell.

BANJER TOWER
PoC 40

Situated on the world of **Vermazen**, the tower in the **Old Market**, **Salou Sain**, is a popular rendezvous point.

BARLEYCORN
SK 55

A planet of the **Rigel Concourse**.

BASINGSTOKE
NL 41

One of the few defining memories of the world of Basingstoke is that I have been told that one can buy candlesticks from a farm on Rijjalooma Ridge.

BELFESER
F 77

It is a major settlement on **Dar Sai**.

BENITRES
F 174

The Broth with Aloe nuts and Water flowers that has become a standard of high cuisine within the Gaean Reach originated at Benitres on the world **Capella VI**.

BERENSKAYA
BD 101

Known only because this place was seen by one Dwyddion as he rose in the Institute. More than that, who knows? Not I.

BERING SEA
PL 57

According to doggerel, or at least the mad poet Navarth, this is the sea, probably on **Earth**, which one must swim in order to woo a dainty Eskimo. Make of it what you will.

BERLIN
PL 47

A city on Europe. Note here the difference of the two usages. A city can be described as being "in" Europe or equally it can be described as being "on" Europe. The former usage considers "Europe" to be some cohesive social entity which exits of its own right, within geographical boundaries. The second considers "Europe" to be little more than a rock and earth raft which exists to conveniently keep the inhabitants from having to adapt to an aquatic condition of life. In the interests of philosophical and linguistic fairness, I will use both usages as seems appropriate or as whim takes me.

BERNAL
SK 150 | KM 34

Known only as the home of the flame fighters and flame-maidens, the inhabitants often wear tight black jackets and white breeches.

BETHUNE PRESERVE
BD 181, 188

The sole life-supporting planet of **Corvus 892**, Bethune Preserve is a strange mixture, a combination of nature reserve, tourist attraction and administrative headquarters for various environmentalist organisations. There are over six hundred game and nature reserves, which range from an entire continent to an acre that supports a solitary lillaw tree. All these reserves are jealously guarded and are maintained in their original state. Travellers arrive on planet at the Special Visitors Compound at **Tanaquil**.

BEYOND
SK 25

The name given to that part of space beyond the **Oikumene** that is not formally policed.

BIRKENHALTER
PoC 75

A canton of the world of **Taubry**.

BIRZUL
KM 115

A princedom on the world of **Thamber**, where the Godmus keeps a harem of ten thousand concubines. Every day he enlists ten new ones and discharges ten old ones.

BISSOM'S END KM 9

A world in the **Beyond**. The fourth planet of Carina LO-461.

BIZE PARISH BARRENS KM 79

A wild area of **Cumberland** (on **Krokinole**, the third largest planet of the **Rigel Concourse**) considered suitable for field-testing all-terrain vehicles, not far from the Crystal Pinnacles.

BLACK BARN F 203

On **Methel**, this **Twanish** nightspot, popular with young people, is close enough to the south of Twanish to be convenient, but far enough away to ensure that you are unlikely to bump into your parents or other respectable persons by accident.

BLACKFORD'S LANDING BD 41

This is a town in **Terranova**, on the world **Denebola V**.

BLAISE AS 326

A star, also known as the Blue-eyed Devil, it is orbited by the planet of **Natrice**.

BLEADSTONE WOODS BD 172

Mentioned by Howard Alan Treesong, but with no other details known.

BLENKINSOP L 136

Also known as **Moulder** 17, the world has two icebound polar continents, four other continents that are sodden marshes with slow rivers, and two inhabited continents with rolling hills in the south. North of the hills are the five cities of the Blenks, and north of them the great industrial yards. The Shimerati, the highest caste of the population, live in palaces along the crests of the hills; the Hummers, who form the professional class, live on the slopes of the highlands in pretentious mansions; whilst the rest live in solid little bungalows along the streets of the towns. There are underground subways, but motorised rickshaws serve as taxis, and old women have pushcarts.

The Trevanian theatre provides the centre of cultured existence, which tells you all that you need to know about Blenkinsop.

BLISSFUL PLAINS F 21

These are on the planet **Verlaren**.

BLUE FOREST CAMP BD 190

This is a camp in the **Grand Triste Primitive Reserve**, on the world **Bethune Preserve**.

BLUE PLANET SK 39

I write here purely because to leave the entry blank looks unprofessional. Thus and so, it is done.

BLURRY CORNERS BD 140

A town comparatively near **Gladbetook** on the planet of **Moudervelt**. It boasts an inn; where, justifiably or not, I cannot comment.

BODELSEY ABBEY KM 26

On **Aloysius**, it is an ancient building, full of antiquities and relics from past times.

BOGARDUS F 195

The world on which the beer Edelfrimpschen is brewed. I suppose it is an adequate reason for remembering a world.

RIVER BOHULOE BD 119

Forms the northern boundary of the **Land of Maunish** on **Moudervelt**.

BONIFACE SK 51 | BD 84

This world circles **Vega**; it is the outermost inhabited world and is gloomy and dank. The oceans know terrible storms, the land seems to know only extremes, either immense plains blasted by wind and rain, or twisted and tortured mountain ranges. Used originally as a penal colony, there are few inhabitable areas and none that afford much comfort. Still, the world is known for the wealth of its quarrymen.

HOTEL BON TON BD 124

The hotel in **Cloutie**, **Moudervelt**.

BORKLAND KM 56

Large continent on **Krokinole**.

BORUGSTONE SK 26

A town notable for the punctilio and gravity of its Grand Sessions, but, alas, its location escapes me.

BOSSOM'S WORLD MT 92

Near the **Great Hole**; Frinsse Junction on Bossom's World is served by a weekly packet which travels to **Eiselbar**.

BOWER MOUNTAINS PL 33

These mountains are on **Murchison**; they slope down to the polar seas and are home to the aboriginal inhabitants who are often hunted.

BRAICHIS SK 51

One of the nineteen independent nations on **Olliphane**. The inhabitants, the Braichish, are headstrong, involute, and considered by others a peculiar people.

BRAMVILLE TOWER BD 12

On St. Paidrigh Square, **Pontefract**; home of *Cosmopolis* magazine.

BRAN PoC 125

Giant star around which circles its third planet, **Terce**.

BRINKTOWN SK 11

Once at the edge of known space, it is now in the North East Middle **Beyond**; its leading inhabitants are virtually all wanted for offences within the **Oikumene**. The town consists of houses set well apart on leafy avenues, and the houses tower above the trees, each a concatenation of turrets, belfries, cupolas, spires, etc.

BRUSE-TANSEL MA 8

Also known as Alastor 1102, population about two hundred thousand, most of whom live around the neighbourhood of Lake Vain, where they work mainly in fabric dying. The most important of the four spaceports is Carfaunge, which also has a hospital and a police "Hall of Inquiry." Indigents are sent out to Gaswin Moor to be paid three-and-a-half ozols a day picking pods for the dye works.

BUDAPEST PL 47

A city on Europe.

BUGTOWN BD 9

A town on **Arcturus IV**.

BUNTER'S SHADE F 129

On the edge of Terwig Waste, on the route from **Serjeuz** to **Dinkelstown**.

BUNTERTOWN BD 152

Probably a small town in Maunish, **Moudervelt**. We say this with some confidence; there are no large towns in Maunish, and calling these places villages or, worse, hamlets merely offends.

BURTON-ON-TRENT PL 44

Town in England where Worthington's brewery still stands.

CADWAL
AS 11

The sole inhabited planet of **Syrene**, it has three continents, **Ecce**, **Deucas** and **Throy**. There is otherwise little of interest unless you like great oceans. There are some other points of land: they are **Lutwen Atoll**, **Thurben Island** and **Ocean Island**, which are all off the east coast of Deucas, and a few rocky islets off Cape Journal in the far south.

At the north pole, at least some of the polar ice floats because an illicit depot was set up, with submarine access and parking for small space-yachts.

CAFFIN'S WORLD
AS 322

A world occasionally visited by Floreste and the **Cadwal** Mummers.

CALASTANG
KM 115

This is a principality on the world of **Thamber**. It is perhaps of interest that the Divine Eye is carried through the city on an altar forty yards long and forty yards high? Or perhaps not.

CALOPSID SEA
KM 45

A shallow sea on **Sasani** (also known as Aquila GB 1201 IV, the home world of **Interchange**).

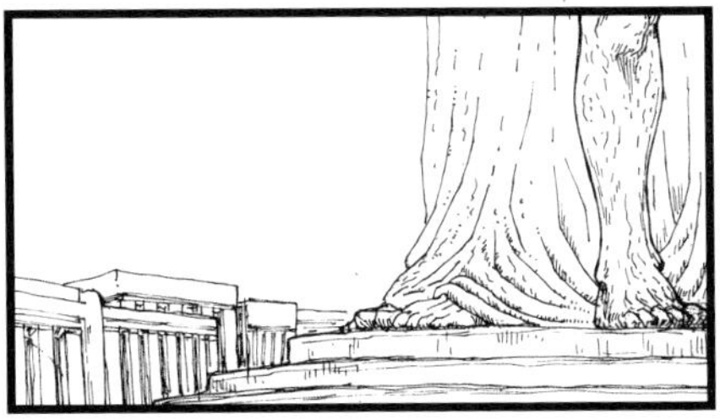

CAMBERWELL
NL 9, 268

The only inhabited world of **Robert Palmer's Star**. There are four continents divided by oceans; the fauna is bizarre, startling and destructive. On two continents the fauna have been left to get on with it, but the other two continents have been set aside for human habitation, and the wildlife is curtailed. The planet was populated from a dozen different sources, and the settlers remain obdurately separate. Tanzig is the most important town, built with concentric rings of buildings facing a central plaza where three one-hundred-foot-high bronze statues stand. Tanzig is ten miles south of the river Bass. Forty miles from Tanzig's dilapidated spaceport is the small town of Sronk; it lies across the Wyching Hills at the edge of the Wildenberry Steppe. The steppe is quite interesting; there are eighteen tribes of Vongo gypsies who roam there. The Foisie River valley runs about thirty miles south of Sronk. Pagg Road runs through the valley.

Point Extase, population four thousand, is five miles down the Foisie River from its nearest point to Sronk.

CAMBIASQ
GE 156

It is the sort of world where a social climber might claim to have an estate. Other than that, I know nothing.

CANOPUS III
BD 149

It exists. Be glad; otherwise we would have to renumber the subsequent Canopus worlds.

CANOPUS IX
T 73

On this planet is Foucher, where failed politicians and abstract political philosophers can dream of retiring to raise fine poultry.

CAPELLA VI
F 174

The planet on which **Benitres**, the home of Broth with Aloe nuts and Water flowers, is situated.

CAPELLA IX
AS 39

The planet on which **Tamar** is situated, of no real interest but safe enough for an elderly grandfather to take a doting grandson for his first space trip.

CAPE MAY
BD 198

A prominent feature on the coast north of **Port Wheary**, **Aloysius**.

CAPH
BD 137

Mentioned in passing, for all I know it could be a planet, a village or a class of Pelecypoda.

CAPH IV
F 84

A lively little world. **Svengay** is there.

CAPRICORN CAFÉ
F 213

On **Methel**, this café overlooks **Redemption Park** half way between the **Commercial Hotel** and **Skohune Tower** in the city of **Twanish**. Actually it is quite reasonably priced for the area and a pleasant enough place to sit and eat.

CARO
SK 161

A planet **Beyond**, whose mayor was kidnapped and tortured by Malagate, one of the Demon Princes. Some worlds are remembered because they produce fine rum, others because their mayor is tortured to death by a brigand with a flair for publicity. One is forced to ponder the nature of fate.

CARRAI
SK 114

A city in **Vadrus** on **Thamber**.

CASHEL CREARY
BD 84

One of the few little towns on **Boniface**, but please don't take that as an encouragement to visit.

CASINO PLAGEALE
SK 133

A night spot in **Avente** near **Les Sirenes**.

CASSIOPEIA
AS 87

It is the sort of place where one's relatives live, but where one would never visit oneself.

CATILINE HILLS
SK 137

A range of hills inland of **Avente**.

CATTLESBURY
BD 101

A town on **Trans-Iskana**, on **Alphanor**.

CAX
PoC 219

This world is the home of the Aquabelle Island work camp.

CELE
BD 82

A beach near **Wild Isle** on the world of **Cytherea Tempestre**. It is pleasant enough for family picnics; it isn't often that you get bodies washed up there.

CENTRAL SHADE
F 89

The central, main shade of **Serjeuz**, the major settlement on **Dar Sai**.

CERVANTES UNIVERSITY
KM 67 | PL 66

Whether named after the man or the place, its location is, alas, lost.

CETI 1620
F 21

Also known as **Fritz's Star**, **Hyaspis** is its fifth planet.

CHAILLES
F 136

An area of desert near **Dinkelstown** on **Dar Sai**, centred round a decayed volcanic crag rising amidst a shoal of ledges and outcrops.

CHAIM
PoC 41

On **Vermazen** this river flows through **Salou Sain** near the **Old Market**.

CHALCEDON
KM 11

A spaceport on **Earth**.

CHAMANITA PLANET
EOE 73

A world to which the Yips from **Cadwal** were to be deported.

CHAM RIVER
F 200

This place is only mentioned in "The Avatar's Apprentice" in *Scroll From the Ninth Dimension*

CHANCY'S TEA HOUSE
BD 9

At the top of **Sailmaker Beach** on **Alphanor**. Reasonably priced, the locals take tea there; it isn't just a tourist trap.

CHLODIE
BD 101

A place on **Marskens**, seen by Dwyddion as he rose in the Institute and where he was arrested. I suppose one can assume Marskens to be a world, but frankly I don't know.

CHRYSANTHE
SK 55

A planet of the **Rigel Concourse**.

CHTHONIAN BOG
SK 186

Perhaps a mythical place, home of the potentially mythical folk of the Chthonian Bog.

CICELY
GE 45

An agricultural world, there are islands in the north, one of which is Huldice, where Thrope can be found. It is a quiet place where nothing much happens save harvest follows seedtime as the seasons change, and they play a genteel hussade. The planet boasts Dagglesby University.

CITY TEN
PL 119

On the planet of **Sogdian**, it is also known as Kouliha. The city is the base for those visiting the Palace of Love.

LAKE CLARE
SK 63

The centre of the most populated area of **Olliphane**.

CLOUTIE
BD 110

Capital of the **Land of Maunish** on **Moudervelt**. Population three thousand.

COMMERCIAL HOTEL
F 177

A reasonably priced hotel (given the location) in **Twanish** on **Methel**.

CONGREVE HOTEL
PL 28

Large hotel in **New Wexford** on **Aloysius**. Like the town itself, the hotel has an aura of good living, law and order, and solid respectability.

CONOVER
SK 43

A town and administrative centre on the world of **Cuthbert**.

COPUS
SK 51, KM 91, BD 19, BD 101, BD 140

A planet circling **Pi Cassiopeia**. The spaceport is known for Fat Hannah who runs a bar there. On Copus are brewed the beers Obladense and Old Subterranean.

Mersilin rugs are made in the **Adar Mountains**. Also small gypsy rugs are made in the **Khajar Realm**.

It was on Copus that the Factors of Pollardich shaved the head of Dwyddion as he rose through the Institute.

If you do visit Copus, whilst you will doubtless be pestered by family to bring back overpriced but remarkably pretty rugs, remember that Mama Potts's Swillery at **Sairle City** serves pepper rum.

CORA
F 21

This star is also known as **Argo Navis 961**; **Dar Sai** is its third planet.

CORFU
PL 98

An island on **Earth**.

CORNU SECTOR NL 9
A sector of the constellation of **Ophiuchus**.

CORPORATION CIRCUIT HOTEL BD 192
This hotel is located at **Blue Forest Camp**, **Bethune Preserve**. It isn't fabulous, but the choice is strictly limited.

CORRIB PLACE BD 33
A street in **Pontefract** Old Town, **Aloysius**, it is paved with granite slabs each hand carved and dovetailed into its neighbours as an act of penance by long-dead monks. On one side is the old Estebanite monastery, now converted into commercial suites. It also has shops offering only goods of distinction and elegance.

CORT TOWER STATION KM 28
The tower block in **Avente** containing the local IPCC offices.

CORVUS 892 BD 188
Part of a system of a dozen other yellow dwarves, with fourteen planets between them. **Bethune Preserve** is the only one to support life.

CREARY CASTLE KM 27
A castle full of antiquities on **Aloysius**.

HOTEL CREDENZA KM 28, SK 82
A hotel in **Avente**, **Alphanor**.

CROY EOE 134
A city on **Earth**.

CUENOS NOTOS F 174
This is the world on which can be found the Oxygen Marshes. These are where the Five-Horned Darango frolics prior to being killed for its cutlets.

CUMBERLAND KM 56
A small continent of **Krokinole**. For the sightseer it is best known for containing the Crystal Pinnacles of Bize Parish and the Card River Falls of Dinker Parish. The continent is also home to the industrious Whitelocks.

CUTHBERT SK 43, BD 83
A planet circling **Vega**. One of the three inhabited worlds, humid and unpleasantly marshy, with few areas comfortably inhabitable; known as the "bug hunters paradise."

CYGNUS T342 SK 53
The star of the planet **Euville**.

CYTHEREA TEMPESTRE BD 41, 44, 106
This planet in Virgo is notable mainly for the fact it is here that one finds **Wild Isle**, a resort. Some might say notorious resort, but I feel it is not necessarily my place to make judgements.

DA'AR-RIZM KM 44
A desert on **Sasani**; the insects are carnivorous, and the autochthonous inhabitants are anthropophages.

DAHANE FOREST BD 170
A forest mentioned by Howard Alan Treesong. Given his temperament, it isn't necessarily evidence that it exists.

DAISY'S LANDING BD 149
A place on **Canopus III**.

DALGLISH RIVER BD 119
Forms the south and east boundaries of Maunish on **Moudervelt**.

DANKWALL TAVERN BD 129
A tavern on the outskirts of **Cloutie**, **Moudervelt**.

DAR SAI
F 21, F 73, F 89, F 113

This is the second planet of **Cora**, **Argo Navis 961** (the third planet is **Methel**), home of the lanslarke, a predacious winged creature. Strangely enough, it is not **Beyond**, but, given the nature of the inhabitants, it might as well be. At the poles the winds create a perpetual down-draught cyclone that deposits on them endless slush and snow. This water drains into the Bogs that fringe each polar region. These are areas of ooze, poisonous slime, and algae so complex as to achieve the size of bushes. As one passes out of the region of the Bogs, one enters the Hot Zone, or Wale, where water either evaporates or sinks into the sand. Cora once had a companion known posthumously as **Fideske**. This companion disintegrated into fragments — the largest is **Shanitra**, the moon of Methel — some fell onto the two worlds. In Methel they disappeared into the oceans, but on Dar Sai these fragments, rich in elements with high atomic numbers, were mixed with the sands and ground down, and, like the sand, they blow endlessly around the planet and collect in lodes of duodecimates. The inhabitants, or **Darsh**, survive by mining the duodecimates. To do this they live in "shades," which are best thought of as enormous parasols, often up to five hundred feet high, shading thirty acres. Water is pumped from the underground aquifers and up the central shaft of the parasol to run down over its surface and fall as a veil to the ground, thus cooling the air within the shade. The Darsh are pretty much of a part with their planet. Harsh, unwilling to concede to the demands of others.

The four main settlements are **Serjeuz**, **Wabber's Fountain**, **Dinkelstown**, and **Belfeser**. There are only rudimentary facilities for spaceship repair, no central Darsh authority, and no restrictions on entering and leaving the planet. Such order as is maintained is maintained by Methlen looking after their own interests.

DARSH
F 22

Pertaining to the inhabitants of **Dar Sai**.

DARTLEY HOLE
PoC 93

Judicial quarry near **Port Tanjee**, where offenders serve their sentences.

DASHBOURNE PLANET
GE 169

The home world of Palladian elms.

DAVID ALEXANDER'S PLANET
F 10

A planet on which the spaceport/city of **Thrump** is situated.

DELIA'S VALE
NL 209

A backwoods planet where spaceships can be robbed and the crews killed at the starport.

DENEBOLA V
BD 41

A world, on which the region of **Terranova** can be found.

DERARD
PoC 16

A world close to **Vermazen**, known for a cycle of bucolic festivals with high-kicking peasant dances and outdoor banquets.

DERDYRA
F 195

The world on which the beer Mahogany Select is brewed.

DESPAZ
KM 120

Main inhabited continent on **Thamber**.

DEUCAS
AS 12

A continent on the world of **Cadwal**, it is the largest and sprawls along the northern temperate zone. The fauna can be savage, even semi-intelligent. The continent is the site of

Araminta Station. Deucas is divided into sixty districts or Lands; Marmion Land, along the coast from Araminta Station, is opposite **Lutwen Atoll**, and Yips tend to cross over and set up camps and have to be ejected.

Southwest of Araminta Station (which is in the foothills of the Muldoon Mountains) is a land of meadows and forests that gives onto the Twan Tivol River, which flows from north to south, ending in the Dankwallow Swamp. The swamp is drained by the **River Wann** and the **River Leur**. Beyond that is savannah. There are then mountains, lakes, forests and rivers, and the land starts to climb to become a wide upland. To the west is a mountain range (the Mandala Mountains) with twenty peaks. Then one comes to the Plain of Moans with Lake Dimple to the west and Mad Mountain straight ahead. Originally, Mad Mountain was known as Mount Stephen Tose. This is where the Banjee migration routes intersect. One route goes north-south, the other east-west. The Mad Mountain lodge is just above the crossing point, with a good view of where the migrating tribes fight at the intersection.

Another notable landmark on Deucas is Cape Tierney Thys, which juts out from the west coast opposite **Ecce**.

DEULLE MA 21

Alastor 2121, where Baruilla acts as a transit port.

DIAMANTHA GP 24

According to the natives, Jennet, the planetary capital, is a dreary city on an unexciting world. Pharmaceuticals are important and may well be the planet's largest export.

DIFFERY DOWNS F 136

An area of desert near **Dinkelstown**.

DIMMICK PoC 54

The chief world of **Maudwell's Star**, Leo JN-44. It has been described, perhaps generously, as a "graceless world, shrouded by a dismal overcast which often condenses to a pall of lugubrious drizzle." There are several theoretically inhabitable continents, but the population lives in the area around the city of **Flajaret**. The oceans are covered in mats of algae a foot thick, which are infested by swarms of insects. The original judicial punishment was to be dressed in boots, a breechclout and a respirator, and placed a metred distance out from the coast on an algae mat. Now this is only done for attacks on IPCC agents, where the offender is released on the very centre of a mat.

DINKELSTOWN F 67

also spelt Dinklestown

A major settlement on **Dar Sai**; when a great hadaul is held, it has five parasols. A place that sums up the **Darsh**: if they cannot be bothered to work out how the name is spelt, they are unlikely to be too worried about town planning.

DIOGENES SK 55

A planet of the **Rigel Concourse** (in Orion).

DIOGENES JUNCTION T 55, 72

It is on the planet Clarence Attic at the base of **Mircea's Wisp** in the constellation of Pegasus. As the name implies, it is a transit point.

DIOSOPHEDE MT 1

It was the fourteen-ship contingent of Credential Renunciators from this world that was the last to colonise **Maske**. The world is urbanised and nature is strictly controlled, indeed regulated. The Diosofids are frivolous, cynical, and addicted to novelty and vicarious emotion. They are notorious for their lack of respect for authority.

DIRTY RED'S BD 149

On the pier at **Daisy's Landing**, **Canopus III**, it is one of the most intolerably drunken dens in the **Oikumene**.

DJANAD MT 3, 8

On **Maske**, south of **Thaery**, the area is now divided into Upper and Lower Djanad, and the inhabitants, the Saidanese, became known as the Djan. They retain their old customs and appear to bear no ill will to those later colonists who conquered much of their land.

The Djan weave rugs of incredible intricacy; a thousand knots per square inch isn't unusual. The rugs are occasionally categorised as "one-life" or "two-life" to indicate the number of lifetimes spent on producing the one rug.

If the Djan are kept in solitude, they can erupt into berserk fury at the slightest provocation, and, if they escape, will haunt the wilderness as cunning and sadistic killers, known as slanes, until they are destroyed.

DOBBIN'S FOUNTAIN F 66

A place on **Dar Sai** near **Gaggar's Shade**.

DOHOBAY MT 3

The region of **Maske** north of the Long Ocean; the tribes are descended, at least in part, from those in the fourteenth colony ship that crashed or was shot down as it tried to leave.

DOMUS F 9

A hotel converted from the temple of St. Revelras, on **Aloysius**.

DORGAN CENTRAL SPACEPORT PL 28

Dorgan is the largest continent on **Aloysius**; the spaceport serves **New Wexford** twenty miles to the north.

DUBHE F 84

Comparatively close to **Caph IV**.

DUGG'S SHADE F 117

A shade between **Serjeuz** and **Jamile Wallow**, on **Dar Sai**, it is a settlement of one parasol. **Darsh** settlements are rated by the number of parasols. Whilst one large parasol might provide more inhabitable area than three lesser ones, three lesser ones provide more security should there be a mechanical problem.

DUNES SPACEPORT BD 28

A few miles south of **Pontefract** on Bottleglass Bay, it is connected to Pontefract by underground rail.

DUPTIS MAJOR BD 30

A world known for its lime trees.

DUSA L 42

A hard little world on the very edge of **Beyond**, with an IPCC post in the town of Wanne. Reputedly the meanest IPCC posting on that side of the Reach.

DUVRAY PoC 214

On **Alcydon**, it is the home of the Pan-Arts Museum.

DWAN WA 9, 24

The sun of **Wyst**, Alastor 1716. As seen from some parts of the **Alastor Cluster**, it is regarded as being in the constellation "the Turtle" on the edge of its carapace, but constellations are subtle and arbitrary depending entirely on the view point of the viewer, thus and so we only mention those constellations as seen from **Earth**.

DYS GE 46

A planet near **Tamar** and **Maz**.

EARTH SK 36 | F 195 | BD 19 | EOE 79, 82, 90, 147, 196, 199, 247, 257

Also **Old Earth**. The ultimate repository of every sort of knowledge, more reasonably it is also the home of the beers Bass Ale, Hinano, Tusker, and Anchor Steam.

Much that is traditional still continues; Persian rugs are still exported, Moldavia is a source of apparently Hellenistic antiques, and even Timbuctoo still exists — to reach it one has to cross the Niger River at Hamshatt Bridge, the Sahara desert remaining a desert.

For spaceports there are Grand Fiamurjes Spaceport, Ybarra spaceport and Tammeola Spaceport, the spaceport for Division City and what was formally known as the American continent.

For the sentimental, Bangalore still exists, as does Lisbon, while at Tanjer one can get a trans-Atlantic sky train to Old Tran, which is in the middle of the American continent, but now known as Division City.

To really see the heart of this continent, from Division city, fly two hundred miles west to Largo on the Sippewissa River. From there, fly north across the Big Prairie to Idola. Fosco Creek is five miles north. These places haven't changed since before humanity went to the stars.

ECCE AS 12

One of the three continents of **Cadwal**, it is on the equator. There are three volcanoes, one of which is dormant; the rest of the continent is a flat terrain of jungle, swamp and morass, with slow-moving rivers languidly making their way to the sea through flora and fauna of savage vitality. The dead volcano Shattorak is in the centre of the continent, and rises two thousand feet above the swamps and jungles. At one point there was a "prison" run by Smonny there. It had a stockade around the summit, which protected the guards from the wildlife. The prisoners slept in tree houses outside the stockade, but as close to the stockade as they could. Others have been exiled there since; there might even be a small inbred population of subsistence peasant hunter-gatherers in the area now.

The Great Vertes River drains the area close to the foot of Shattorak and, for those with appropriate technology, is a way into the heart of the continent.

EDMONTON PL 100

It is in Canada, on **Earth**, and the goal of the pilgrims seeking the Sacred Shin.

EISELBAR MT 92, MT 100

Circling the yellow giant Bhutra, Eiselbar is a Gaean world near the **Great Hole** in the constellation of Quincunx. The population is gregarious and egocentric; everything has a specific price, nothing is free, and a child incurs a birth-debt that must be repaid to its parents. The economy is based on tourism and the chemical industry; the planet is inhabited by mobile slimes, which synthesise many compounds otherwise impossible to produce and that serve as catalysts for many important reactions. The roads and walkways on the planet tend to be elevated so the slimes pass underneath.

The people tend to wear their own sound-producing devices which play quiet music in time with their thoughts and actions.

Kyash is the main city and spaceport. There are also many tourist lodges. From

Ririjin Lodge a toboggan slide descends along a twenty mile route to the Openlands Resort, at the Priest's Diadem, a system of lakes in the Great Salt Desert where the "Nineteen Naughty Naiads perform their unique and mirth provoking underwater Ballet," whilst the Gardens of Paradise, raised on glass stilts above the desert, are also worth visiting.

ELFLAND — SK 55

A planet of the **Rigel Concourse**.

ELLENT — TA 52

Alastor 485, the home of the Boles, a predominantly left-handed people who are deeply religious and will not eat fish.

EPSILON SAGITTAE — F 21

A star also known as **Komred**.

ERDIC REALMS — WA 44

The extent of humanity is divided into four areas, the **Alastor Cluster**, the Gaean Reach, the Erdic Realms, and the **Primarchic**. Nothing further is known about the Erdic, but I would assume it was a lesser swarm of stars, smaller and even further away from the galaxy than the Alastor Cluster.

ERGARD — L 28

Ergard is a congested world, remarkable, if at all, for the world city of Coreon. It was from amongst its population that the colonists who settled **Fluter** were drawn.

ERIDU — PL 68

According to Navarth it was the home of the beautiful Zan Zu. We know nothing else. Given Navarth this may be an outright lie, a romantic fiction, or even the truth. It might be the last (by no means impossible; it has been pointed out that even Navarth had to tell the truth occasionally, if only to ensure that tradesmen delivered to the correct address), but still it should be noted that Eridu is reputedly the oldest of the Sumerian cities, and Navarth, perhaps familiar with the *Epic of Gilgamesh*, would be familiar with the name.

ESPANDENCIA — BD 48

A town on **Algenib IX**.

ESPLANADE — SK 135 | F 26

Also the "Grand Esplanade." This road is the centre of fashionable — and, to a lesser extent, unfashionable — **Avente** life. That being said, it must be remembered that many cities in the Concourse have one, although never with as much zest. There again, even for Avente, the Esplanade becomes Pilkamp Road when it reaches the city of **Rath Eileann**. Let that be a lesson in humility for all of us.

ESTREMONT — F 11

On a **Lake Feamish** islet, it is part of **Rath Eileann** and is one of the places in the Vegan system in which the Court of Interworld Equity sits three times a year under a Circuit Propounder.

ETA OPHIUCHI — KM 30

This is the alternative name for the star **Sabik**.

ETRURIA — SK 56

One of the seven nearly contiguous continents on **Alphanor**.

ETTENHEIM — PoC 168

The home of Ettenheim Spaceyards? In all candour, Ettenheim could be a planet, a town, or even the company's founder. I draw no conclusions.

EUVILLE — SK 53

This world circles **Cygnus T342**; it is a planet that has an "unpleasant and psychotic" population who live in five cities, Oni, Me, Che, Dune, and Ve. Each is built in pentagonal patterns around a five-sided citadel. The spaceport, on a remote island, is known as "Orifice." Passports are not available; visitors must have a star tattooed on their foreheads, one for each city they wish to visit, a different colour for each city (orange, black, mauve, yellow, and green). Casual visitors are rare.

FADER NL 220, 312

This world goes in orbit around the star **Night Lamp**. It has two moons. It is a world so remote it isn't in the *Handbook to the Planets*, but it is not too far from the Yellow Rose system. Spaceport is at Flad. The Roum, who represent the largest single market worth serving, live at Romarth, the city in the forest.

The single continent occupies much of the southern hemisphere, with an ocean covering the rest. The continent has a central forest, known as Blandy Deep, with steppe on all four directions. Flad is in the middle of the northern steppe. There is a railway connecting Romarth and Flad crossing the Tangtsang Steppe passing under the Beresford Bluffs. Once in the forest, the train halts at the Skein River where passengers take to a barge which sails through the forest to Romarth.

Romarth is centred on the Gamboye Plaza, from which the residential boulevards are to the north. Carleone Palace is on the plaza. The principle avenue, the Esplanade, leads past Gamboye Plaza where the Foundance stands huddled over the water. The Foundance is where new Seishanee (servants in quasi-human form who are built in vats) are created.

FALLORNE GE 76

A world on the far side of the Reach.

FANUCHE GE 83

A planet. There you are; a definitive statement, no equivocation, no quibbling. Admittedly not a lot of use, unless you are someone who persistently enters pub quizzes run by quizmasters of superior peculiarity, but, still, one cannot have everything in this world.

FAR EDGE BD 9

A world reputedly at the edge of the **Oikumene** (as in the phrase "from Far Edge to **Tangiers Old Socco**"; as Tangiers is on **Earth**, this range is probably cultural and sociological rather than just cartographical.

FAREWELL STATION F 174

Known for its Dumplings of Belsifer Root with Saffron. It is on the world of **Miriotes**.

LAKE FEAMISH F 6

A lake in Llinliffet's Land on the world of **Aloysius**.

THE FENS TA 14

A district of remarkable beauty on **Trullion**; thousands of waterways split the area into innumerable islands, some so small they barely support a cabin and a tree from which to tie the boat. Some are large enough for villages; the inhabitants get everywhere by boat, and there is a ferry which connects **Welgen** with the villages. In the centre of the Fens is Rabendary Island, a few miles from the village of Saurkash. There is, if sundry minions manage a modicum of competence, a map to further illustrate this area.

FERRIER'S CLUSTER SK 161

A sector of the **Beyond** including over a hundred settlements on at least a similar number of planets.

FERRISTOUN DISTRICT SK 65

A dismal district of **Sansontiana**, the second city of **Olliphane**, it is notable for its endless warehouses enlivened by cheerfully carved and ornamented little taverns somehow inserted amongst them.

FIAME SK 50

A planet in the **Rigel Concourse**.

FIAMETTA PoC 165, 174

A world with three moons that orbits the sun **Kaneel Verd**. On it you will find the town of Girandole, of moderate size with central market place; the houses are bungalows with verandas, second floor galleries, high-peaked roofs, built of dark wood.

It is also the locale of the Moabite Cloudlands. These are a hundred miles east of Girandole, where there are rocky crags and high meadows where jade was once mined, and the last descendants of the mine owners have withdrawn into themselves to become a psychically disturbing people. Below the Cloudlands there is the old town of Zemerle, the only safe place to look for artefacts from the region.

There is also Sweetfleur, home of the Grand Lalapalooza (a giant funfair), where one can stay at the Green Star Inn. Of special interest to tourists, near the Botanic Mountains, there is River-Isle, where the clowns will use a mélange of instruments to make a noise until they get ten sols to go away.

FIDDLETOWN BD 84

One of the few little towns on **Boniface** with nothing to recommend it, so I will discuss it no further.

FIDESKE F 73

A dead companion star of **Cora**. It split into fragments, some of which formed an asteroid belt, some of which formed **Methel**'s moon and some of which fell onto **Dar Sai** where they form lodes in the shifting sand.

FITLINGASSE PL 58

A narrow grey alley off Boulevard Castel Vivence. In Fitlingasse, there is a dock, decaying, with a couple of houseboats and a saloon. It is on one of these houseboats that Navarth used to live. Effectively part of **Ambeules**.

FLAJARET PoC 55

On the world of **Dimmick**, the city of Flajaret has little to recommend it unless you particularly like dogfighting. It is the service centre of mines in the locality. Hotel Apollon is the safest place for an off-worlder to eat.

FLAMANDE HEIGHTS PL 69

The site of the ancient cathedral that looks over **Ambeules**, a suburb of **Rolingshaven** on the west coast of Europe.

FLESSELRIG NL 259

On this world the city of Ocknow, capital and spaceport, is the commercial and financial node serving much of the back sector.

FLOIRY PLACE PoC 40

In **Salou Sain**, north of the **Old Market**.

FLUTER PoC 296 | L 26

This world circles the star **Frametta**. It is a tranquil world with pleasant scenery and few natural hazards. It is known as a world of one hundred rivers. Coro-coro Spaceport (on Continent Five) has Pomare Boulevard, which leads to the O-Shar-Shan Hotel (the best hotel but with no running hot water), with hotels, agencies, shops, taverns (among which is Pingis Tavern) and residences along the route.

The Maudlen Moors nearby provide a pleasant walk.

The planet has nine narrow continents running north-south in the northern hemisphere; the southern hemisphere is one huge ocean. The population lives in scattered villages; the planetary population is fixed at 999,000.

For tourists seeking a safe holiday away from the other tourists, Krenke is one of the villages we could recommend; the Three Feathers provides excellent lodging for tourists. The Mellamy Steeps are a wild area close by, well worth a look.

On the second continent is the river Suametta, an especially fine anchorage for a houseboat. It is near the village Pengelly which boasts the Iron Crow Inn. Both would fit well into the itinerary of the tourist who wishes for a leisurely time spent in placid surroundings.

FOMALHAUT PLANETS SK 120

They are known for their ruins which predate humanity.

FORESSE SK 7

Foresse is on the planet **Krokinole**; it is notable mainly as the place where the Ecclesiarchic Nunciamento of Year 1000 was published. There, never let it be said we do not inculcate an interest in culture and spirituality.

FOTHERINGAY SHADE F 117

A shade between **Serjeuz** and **Jamile Wallow**. A settlement of three parasols.

FOUR WINDS BD 48

A place on **Alphanor**; whether pleasant or otherwise, I leave for others to determine.

FRAMETTA PoC 296

Known to poets and advertising executives as "Golden Frametta," it is the star of **Fluter**.

FRITZ'S STAR F 21

Also known as **Ceti 1620**; **Hyaspis** is the fifth planet.

FROGTOWN PITS F 34

I have been assured that this is some sort of **Aloysius** penal institution; perhaps if readers having experienced the joy of this establishment could contact us, we could give a definitive answer.

GAAS PL 39

A European river reaching the sea at **Rolingshaven**.

GAGGAR'S SHADE F 65

One of the lesser shades on **Dar Sai**.

GALLINGALE NL 10

This is the world that houses the Thanet Institute and its College of Aesthetic Philosophy. For those interested in moving, there is considerable new housing planned on the plot of land that was once Merriehew, the rambling old farmhouse. It is four miles north of Thanet; Langolen is the local school. The Institute Health Services are based in Buntoon House.

The local population strives to achieve through a network of clubs and societies; one such club is the Palindrome. One's social status is measured by one's club and one's ranking within it. For families with older offspring, the Lyceum is the upper school and college.

Other suburbs that might interest you are Catterline, apparently convenient for the Institute but certainly not regarded as appropriate for senior Institute people, and

Chermond Park Estates, which is somewhat more select. For social life, the Old Den is a quiet bar popular with young couples. The Conservatory is at the back of Pingaree Park, beside the Vax Memorial. The park is on the foothills of Mount Vax, whilst the Mountain Lake Lodge is also popular with a certain type of clientele.

The Blue Moon Inn (halfway between the space terminal and Thanet) is a useful rendezvous for those not wishing to make a social statement.

To find Merriehew, take Flammarion Prospect from the Institute.

GAMMA ERIDANI F 21

This is the sun of **Reis**, an inhabited world and the sixth planet.

GANNET'S SHADE F 117

A deserted shade between **Serjeuz** and **Jamile Wallow**, a settlement of one parasol, which perhaps explains why so many shades attempt to have at least two parasols.

GARDENA KM 56

A small continent on **Krokinole**, the **Highlands** of Gardena are inhabited by the "Imps," and Mount Jovah, at 42,102 feet, is the highest peak on any of the Concourse planets.

GARDEN OF DIDO T 93

This is where Calyactus, Oomphaw of the Yips, mysteriously died. It is probably on **Rosalia**, but there are no details I would wish to recall for this august publication and its select and cultured readership.

GARREU KM 31

Garreu is the most isolated province of **Scythia** on **Alphanor**, lying between the Mystic Ocean and the **Morgan Mountains**.

GAUDE PHODELIUS IV AS 219

This world is home to the Laddakees. They have squat physiques, fresh complexions, round faces and distinctive wide-brimmed hats with trailing black ribbons.

GEIDION AS 304

As in "you might as well ask me for the moons of Geidion." One assumes it exists, but then one assumes many things equally improbable.

GEMINI 333 IV EOE 98

This world is the home of the bog-runners. For all the good it does it.

GENTILLY KM 113

A province on the world of **Thamber**, it is on the western shore of the smallest continent; it is a peaceful part of the world. In the capital Draszane, there are four ancient colleges and hundreds of small bookshops.

GERLPERINO'S SALOON SK 155

A drinking place in **Melnoy Heights** near **Avente**.

GHNARUMEN SK 131

The Star Kings' name for their home planet. It is comparatively **Earth**-like.

GIETERSMOND GE 181, GE 187

One of the "**Sister Planets**," it houses a technical institute. Narghuys is the spaceport and capital; the Cosmolux Hotel on Prater Huss Square is recommended. The world produces engineers and craftsmen and is not normally considered as a holiday destination. But if you are on the world already and fancy a break in an area where things go more slowly, Jamus Amaha is the wildest area on the planet with jungles at its heart, beyond the Southern

Torpeltines; Masmodo is the main town of Jamus Amaha.

To travel there from Narghuys, ride south by airship to Jonder at the head of the Great Fish River, then join a local connector that stops at every community along the Malabar Littoral, and get off at Cape Jaun, thence to Paunt on Kletterer Island by ocean skimmer. This leads you to the Torpeltines, a series of rocky hulks and spires surrounded by a fringe of beach and a few hundred yards of foliage. About half are inhabited. From Paunt, hire an air-car to fly down the chain of islands to Jamus Amaha; Masmodo is the principle settlement, with the Great Western Hotel, three taverns, warehouses, a hospital/dispensary and boatyards. Dongg's Tavern is at the southern end of the wharves and is probably worth patronising. For unusual sights, Sanctissimus Island used to be a Corrective Institute, whilst at one point there was some sort of illegal research establishment on Tinkum's Bar, which is another of the islands in the locality.

GILBERT'S GREEN STAR — T 73

In **Mircea's Wisp**, this star has eight planets; the inhabited one is **Yaphet**.

GLADBETOOK — BD 110

Capital of Fluter Township in the **Land of Maunish** on **Moudervelt**. The population is three thousand; it lies on the banks of the **Wiggal River**.

GLAMFYRE — GE 7

A rather bleak planet at the edge of the Reach; the town of Ultimo is there.

GLENTLIN — MT 2

The Glentlin is a rocky peninsula to the west of **Thaery**, to which the crew of the thirteenth colony ship were exiled for theological differences. They adapted to their harsh land: some residents in the High Marcatives became bandits raiding into the districts of Thaery; others took to the sea, sailing the long ocean. Eventually the raiding grew too irritating, and the Thariots retaliated to Glint raiding by hiring Saidanese warriors (known locally as perrupters). Glint effectively became a thirteenth district of Thaery.

The northwest tip of Glentlin, from Cape Junchion to the Hacksnaw Hills, was Droad Land.

GORGON RIVER — BD 223

Near the Blue River Outstation, **Bethune Preserve**.

GOSHEN — SK 55

A planet of the **Rigel Concourse**.

GOSHEN PRAIRIE — BD 111

A prairie in the eastern midlands of the only continent on **Moudervelt**.

GRABHORNE — SK 161

A planet in **Ferrier's Cluster** where Malagate maintained slave factories.

GRAND INTERPLANETARY SPACEPORT — SK 58

This huge spaceport serves **Avente**.

GRAND MURCHISON HOTEL — PL 33

It is the main hotel of **Sabra** on **Murchison**, thus it competes with Wilhelm's Trade Hotel, Cady's Tavern and the Blue Ape Hotel. Take your pick; I would not like to be blamed for the temporary inadequacies of any I chanced to recommend.

GRAND POMADOR HOTEL — SK 76

A hotel in **Sansontiana**, second largest city on **Olliphane**.

GRAND TRISTE PRIMITIVE RESERVE — BD 190

One of the big reserves on **Bethune Preserve**.

GRAY WORLD — TA 28

Alastor 1740. To end the reign of Mad King Zag, the Whelm sent in one thousand Tyrant dreadnought warships and landed twenty million heavy infantry on the same day; the

Mad King's militia, stunned by the sheer enormity of the situation, just gave up.

GREAT BULDUKE RIVER BD 191

On **Bethune Preserve**, the river basin is half-a-million square miles, and includes the Blue Forest.

THE GREAT HOLE MT 1

The eastern fringe of the Gaean Reach contains an area known as "The Great Hole." The eastern boundary of the Great Hole is the **Zangwill Reef**. In the very centre of the Great Hole is the star **Mora** with its two worlds, **Maske** and **Skay**.

GREAT SWOMEY RIVER BD 129

About half way between **Cloutie** and **Gladbetook** on **Moudervelt**.

GROARY'S TAVERN F 47

A tavern on the edge of the **Darsh** community, on the shores of **Lake Feamish** in **Wigaltown**, **Rath Eileann**.

HALKSHIRE HOTEL KM 68

A hotel in **Patris**, the Whitelock capital on **Krokinole**.

HALUCE SK 133

A night spot in **Avente** near **Les Sirenes**. Probably frequented by a "faster" set than our readers would feel comfortable with.

HANNAH'S HEAD BD 198

On the coast north of **Port Wheary**, **Aloysius**, it is popular with tourists for the romantic sunset views across to Port Wheary. But then tourists are easily pleased.

HARDACRES SK 55

A planet of the **Rigel Concourse**.

HAUNTED RIVER BD 191

It joins the **Lesser Bulduke River** in the marshes below **Blue Forest Camp**.

STATION HEDRICK PL 58

A subway station on Boulevard Castel Vivence in **Ambeules** beside the **Gaas** estuary.

HIGHLANDS KM 70

The Highlands region of the continent of **Gardena** on **Krokinole** is often referred to just as "The Highlands" without further elaboration. It is the home not merely of the human subspecies the Highland Imp but also the noxious roof-runner, a segmented worm with many legs.

HOPLAND KM 56

Hopland is one of the continents of **Krokinole**; the Druid Banquers wander the northern tundras.

HOUL MUSEUM KM 26

Another old building stuffed full of the antiquities of **Aloysius**, with too little security, and, if you ask me, carrying far too much insurance.

HUNCKERTOWN TRABBLE BD 94

One of the ridges in the Pritz badlands, **Boniface**, where there is a lode of palladium.

HUTT F 201

From "The Avatar's Apprentice" in *Scroll From The Ninth Dimension*.

HYASPIS F 21

The fifth planet of **Fritz's Star**.

IDORA KM 70

The planet Idora, more properly known as Sadal Suud XI, is the home of a thirty-foot-long segmented waterworm. Well, every planet has to be known for something.

IMAGE SK 55

A planet of the **Rigel Concourse**.

IMBER MA 21

In Alastor, you change at Calypso Junction on Imber when travelling from **Deulle** to **Numenes**.

INKIN'S SHADE F 112

Many of the Fogle Clan live at this shade on **Dar Sai**.

INTERCHANGE KM 45

On the planet **Sasani**, this complex acts as a broker for kidnap victims and kidnappers; it is set on a rocky hillock in the **Da'ar-Rizm** desert.

IRTA BD 30

A world known for its frozen tundra. Ask yourself this, would you prefer to hail from a world known for its frozen tundra or for its thirty-foot-long segmented waterworms?

ITCHY NOLA'S SHADE F 129

On the edge of Terwig Waste, on the route from **Serjeuz** to **Dinkelstown**.

JACK CHANDLER'S GULF GE 7

A region of space. Not precisely located.

JAMILE WALLOW F 117

A mining camp some distance from **Serjeuz** on **Dar Sai**.

JAPAN BD 12

On **Earth**; it is perhaps best known as a source of antique earthenware lamps.

JERMIN BAY KM 37

Located on **Alphanor**, Jermin Bay is a bay of the Mystic Ocean. **Garreu** Province is on the shores.

JEZEBEL SK 55

A planet of the **Rigel Concourse**.

JINGKENS STAR GE 175

The star of of **Wittenmond** and its **Sister Planets**.

JINGLES EOE 258, 261

A region of space that extends beyond **Anthony Pringle's World** to the edges of the Reach and to **Nion**. It is a region of bright and dim stars, gas balls, dark scoriated hulks, sullen spheroids of neutron metal, orphan planets, and orphan moons.

JODISEI CONVERSATION AND FLOWER ARRANGING CLUB SK 39

In spite of its name, and the demure appearance of the building, it is reliably reported to us that this establishment, the cultural heart of **Brinktown**, is actually a bordello. Admittedly a well-run and discrete bordello, but still a bordello.

JOHN PRESTON'S WORLD AS 39

They run bus tours out of the seven cities there. Which seems to indicate that there is something to see, but, perhaps in this case, truth and beauty exist only in the eye of the bus-tour guide?

JUNIFER RIVER BOGLANDS BD 129

North of **Cloutie** on **Moudervelt**.

KANDASPE WA 136

A planet close enough to **Zeck** for the inhabitants of both to feel like neighbours when they meet up and are a long way from home.

KANEEL VERD PoC 167

Known as the green star, it is the sun of the planet **Fiametta**.

KARS T 140

Also known as Perseus TT-652-IV. Pasch on Kars is a business centre and serves as a junction point for a dozen major trans-galactic carriers. It is also the hub of a hundred or so feeder routes to everywhere in the Perseid sector.

South of Pasch is Ballyloo Township, the site of L-B Construction's private terminal.

KAW DOON BD 84

One of the few little towns on **Boniface**.

KHAJAR REALM BD 19

On **Copus**, a source of small gypsy rugs.

KIEV PL 47 | EOE 122. 139

A city on **Europe**, on the edge of the great Altaic Steppe, home of the Funusti Memorial Museum. The museum is in the precincts of the old Konevitsky Palace on Murom Hill at the back of Kiev's old town. If you want a good hotel, then the Mazeppa Hotel, with rooms overlooking Prince Bogdan Yurevich Kolsky Square, is probably for you. The "square" is actually a pentagonal area, with two cathedrals and a monastery in Old Slavic style forming three of the sides.

If you decide to walk around Kiev, Sorka Boulevard runs from the square, north along the Dnieper to the museum. For the even more adventurous, there is the Spice Merchants' quarter, and the Mercery. There are many "student bars" in the Spicemerchants' Quarter, the Bobadil, the Nym, Lena's and Dirty Edvard's, the Stone Flower (famous for its cockroaches), and the Universo. Lena's Bistro has the best cabbage rolls, but, for the audacious, there are the Spasm, Mopo's, Suzdal and the Convolvulus. In Suzdal the intellectual climate is as stiff as the weather.

KILLARNEY KM 30

The **Vega** system's penal satellite.

KINDUNE SK 58

Perhaps the largest city on **Olliphane**, on the shores of **Lake Clare**, it has a spaceport which also serves **Sansontiana** eighty miles away, to which it is connected by subway.

POINT KITTERY BD 198

On the coast north of **Port Wheary**, **Aloysius**.

KNOBKELLY ROW F 66

A place on **Dar Sai** near **Gaggar's Shade**.

KODAIRA PoC 17

Home of the Exxil pool which is supposed to contain the fountain of youth. In reality Kodaira does not exist and is part of a marketing scam for the world of **Naharius**, which attempts rather desperately to attract the gullible to partake of its healing waters. Fools, unlike publishers, are soon parted from their money!

KOMRED F 21

Star also known as **Epsilon Sagittae**.

KORYPHON GP 5

On the continent Uaia, a people known as the Uldras inhabit a wide band along the southern littoral known as the Alouan. To the north the Wind-runners sail their two- and three-masted wagons along the Palga plateau. There are depots, but the Wind-runners refuse to allow anyone to fly over their plateau; many families have "light-cannons" with which they all attempt to shoot down any intruder.

South of Uaia across the Persimmon Sea is the equatorial continent of Szintarre whose population comes from off-world. It is in the in the city of **Olanje** on Szintarre that the Mull, the organ of government for the whole planet of Koryphon, resides. The populace of Uaia ignores it, and it tends to ignore them.

A third population on Uaia are the land-barons, whose ancestors, two centuries ago, were off-world freebooters who captured a conclave of Uldra chieftains and forced them to concede large tracts of land which became the great "domains" of the Alouan.

Morningswake Manor, next to the Chipchap River, is perhaps typical. Its territory is considerable, running up to the edge of the plateau and the Volwode mountains near to where the river Mellorus runs in its wide valley.

There are two alien races, considered quasi-intelligent, the erjins and the morphotes.

KOTOP
BD 101

A place seen by Dwyddion as he rose in the Institute. Dwyddion, self absorbed and inward looking, has begun to irritate me; try getting any meaningful details out of him. Frankly, if he is the best the Institute can produce, then there is perhaps hope for the rest of us yet.

KOTZASH WAREHOUSE
F 43

The Kotzash warehouse at **Serjeuz** on **Dar Sai** was robbed in a daring robbery.

KROKINOLE
SK 7 | KM 56

The third largest planet of the **Rigel Concourse**, it is sometimes considered the most beautiful. Krokinole has become a home for many minor races; amongst them are the Arcadians, Batthalese, Singhels, Oporto Fishermen, Jansenists and Ancient Alans.

KUSSINES
PL 84

A village twenty miles east of **Ambeules** on **Earth**, it consists of ancient buildings on the side of a lake.

KYASH
MT 102

Kyash is the main city and spaceport of the world **Eiselbar**. The preferred hotel, especially if travelling on expenses, is the Gandolfo, which is considered absolutely luxurious.

KYRIL
PoC 102

A pilgrim world, with three dim moons, it is the destination of the Clantic Sect. The spaceport is Impy's Landing. The pilgrims' way circumnavigates the world, across acrid wastes, dunes, bogs, moors, and rolling savannahs, with occasional inns and shelters. In the far west is the Holy Mountain, a dying volcano that all must climb; the crater still bubbles with red-hot lava. Halfway round the lip of the volcano is a lookout platform that goes over the magma.

LADAQUE-ROYALE
NL 177

Technically Sagittarius FFC 32-DE-2930. The Groaning Ocean runs up against the Central Massif of the Second Continent, at the Pittispasian Cliffs. The human kites and wind wizards of the cliffs are fascinating.

LAKHME VERDE
NL 127

This is the world on which may be found the Baneek Isles. Each village supports its own Tymanghese orchestra, using waterbells, sound-spangles and gongs to produce "music" said to sound like the surge and retreat of the surf.

LAMBDA GRUS III
SK 11

The home planet of the "Star Kings."

LAND OF AMABLE
BD 119

To the north of the **Land of Maunish** on **Moudervelt**.

LAND OF DINKLAND
BD 123

The inhabitants of the land of Maunish regard Maunish as a haven of tolerance compared to Dinkland.

LAND OF ERQUHAR
BD 119

To the east of the **Land of Maunish** on **Moudervelt**.

LAND OF GANASTER
BD 119

Also to the east of the **Land of Maunish** on **Moudervelt**.

LAND OF LELANDER
BD 110

Three hundred miles south of the **Land of Maunish** on **Moudervelt**.

LAND OF MALCHIONE
BD 123

The inhabitants of the **Land of Maunish** also regard Maunish as a haven of tolerance compared to Malchione. That being said, the inhabitants of the Land of Maunish are hardly unbiased in these matters.

LAND OF MAUNISH
BD 110

This land controls a section of the **Goshen Prairie** on **Moudervelt**.

LAND OF PUCK
BD 119

To the west of the **Land of Maunish** on **Moudervelt**.

LANTANGO PENINSULA
SK 115

A peninsula on **Singhal Island** on **Ys**, a planet of the **Rigel Concourse**.

LAST CALL
BD 149

Regarded as the far extent of space as in "from **Earth** to Last Call."

LATHCAR
KM 115

A province on **Thamber** where the gentry breed slave runners to compete in the Lath Race Meets.

LAYLAND
KM 56

A small continent on **Krokinole**.

LECK
BD 132

A small town near **Gladbetook**, **Moudervelt**.

LENCILORQUA
F 21

A village of 657 inhabitants on **Vasselona** Continent, **Reis**, sixth planet to **Gamma Eridani**.

LENSLE ERG
F 21

A desert. Alas that it was never considered necessary to mention where this desert might be found. Pah, and they call me capricious!

LESSER BULDUKE RIVER
BD 191

A tributary of the **Great Bulduke River**, **Bethune Preserve**.

LES SIRENES
SK 129

A romantic place near the coast, close by **Avente**.

RIVER LEUR
AS 13

Flows through **Araminta Station** of **Cadwal**.

LEVANT
PL 82

A region on **Earth**.

LILIANDER'S HOME
AS 286

This is one of the worlds on the usual circuit of the **Cadwal** Mummers. The circuit is known to visit dull worlds where it does not take a great deal to amuse the populace; hence, it is rare that anywhere on the circuit is worth visiting.

LILLING
PoC 11

A bucolic village on the pleasant world of **Vermazen**.

LINSIL ORQ
F 21

A lake of the **Blissful Plains**, Verlaren. Verlaren is second planet to **Komred**, also known as **Epsilon Sagittae**.

LISSAM
F 201

From "The Avatars Apprentice" in *Scroll From The Ninth Dimension*.

LIVERSTONE
SK 50

On **Fiame**. It is one of the places where Model 9B spaceships are made.

LLALARKNO
F 139

A suburb of **Twanish** on the world of **Methel**, it has a population of about twenty thousand and only Methlen can live there.

LLANFELFAIR
SK 133

A night spot in **Avente** near **Les Sirenes**.

LONDON
SK 119

A city on **Earth**, home of the magazines *Academia* and *Cosmopolis*.

THE LONG HILLS
BD 101

A place seen by Dwyddion as he rose in the Institute. Did I mention Dwyddion before? I think I did; I shall hold my tongue.

LONG PARADE
BD 48

In **Espandencia** on **Algenib IX**.

LORGAN
KM 99

The planet on which Boomaraw College is situated. Note that whilst not perhaps in the front rank of academic institutions, Boomaraw College is not to be sneered at.

LOSASSO TUNNEL
KM 21

On the **Route Slideway** near **Avente**.

LOST STAR INN
SK 133

A night spot in **Avente** near **Les Sirenes**.

LOTHAR PARISH
PL 49

A parish in **Ambeules**, the site of the Philidor Bohus Lyceum.

LUBLINKEN COLLEGE
PL 133

It may be on **Lyonesse**. The sources are deliberately vague; I suspect they don't know either!

MT. LUCASTA
BD 94

A peak on one of the ridges in the **Pritz** badlands, **Boniface**.

LULCHION'S MOUNTAIN RESORT
PoC 15

On the planet of **Vermazen**; known for its fresh air.

LUPUS 2311
PL 53

On this world, the inhuman natives of Peninsula 4A devote the greater part of their lives working on carefully carved stone slabs, and, twice a year at the solstice, exactly 224 are placed on a ceremonial barge that is allowed to drift out onto the ocean, where it is collected by the Lupus Salvage Company, who remove the slabs and sell them as objets d'art.

LUSBARREN
GE 32

At Vaire, just off the Dal coast on Lusbarren, you can make a fortune trawling for angelfish, which you sell to **Banacre**. Trust me, if I knew where Lusbarren was, I'd be out there for the angelfish.

LUSITANIA
SK 56

One of the seven nearly contiguous continents on **Alphanor**.

LUTUS
GE 190

A planet settled by Gettucks, a swarthy and ill-favoured people, it is the home of the Convent of the Divine Prism at Blenny, once raided by the starmenter Yane Cargus.

LUTWEN ATOLL
AS 14

Three hundred miles northeast of **Araminta Station** on **Cadwal**, the atoll has been settled by Yips, the descendants of runaway servants, illegal immigrants and others. On Cadwal the Yips cannot breed with other humans and are considered a subspecies, but this lack of fertility may be due to some constituent in the diet, as Yips on other planets have been able to raise families with local women.

LYCIA
SK 56

One of the seven nearly contiguous continents on **Alphanor**.

LYDIA
SK 56

One of the seven nearly contiguous continents on **Alphanor**.

LYONNESSE
SK 55

A planet of the **Rigel Concourse**. It is the home of the monumental Gnome Iron Works.

MADAGASCAR
SK 55

A planet of the **Rigel Concourse**.

MADERA
BD 74

Home of the Madera Technical College. Madera is a city in and the county seat of Madera County, California, on **Earth**.

MAHRAB
PL 122

The place where unsatisfactory children are sold to, when paid as taxes in **City Ten** on the planet of **Sogdian**.

MAIDHOUSE
AS 32

This world is the sole source of Maidhouse crystals, much valued for jewellery.

MANINGUEZ PLAIN
F 200

From "The Avatar's Apprentice" in *Scroll From The Ninth Dimension*.

LAKE MAR
T 141

Where the mermaids sing; nothing else is known. Frankly, I suspect unscrupulous tourist brochures, but, if so, they are not merely unscrupulous but inept, as they give no details as to on which world Lake Mar might be found.

PORT MAR
MA 65

The main settlement on **Marune**. In Port Mar, Rhunes patronise the Royal Rhune Hotel. In the New Town is the Port Mar College of Arts and Technics has almost ten thousand students, none of them Rhunes.

From the spaceport, the Avenue of Strangers runs into Port Mar; as one travels along, the first stop is the Traveler's Inn, the second, the Outworld Inn, the third, the Royal Rhune Hotel, then over the bridge into New Town for the Cassander Inn and the University Inn. By the bridge the narrow Street of Brass Boxes moves gradually uphill; the shops are old, and the street leads into a square surrounded by curio shops and book shops, etc. From the square, you can leave via the Avenue of Black Jangkars passing through an arched portal into the Royal Rhune Hotel.

New Town has four streets paralleling the river, the Estrada which terminates at the university, the Avenue of the Agency, then the Avenue of Haune and the avenue of Douaune.

In the Fairy Gardens, one can watch performances; one walks up Jibberee Hill to get to the Royal Rhune Hotel.

MARCATIVE MOUNTAINS
MA 4

On **Maske**, they form the boundary between **Thaery** and **Djanad**, and to the west become **Glentlin**.

MARHAB SIX
BD 15

New Concept is the planet circling this star in the middle reaches of Aries.

MARIAH
PoC 241, 272, 285

This world has four continents spaced around the equator. Alpha is bleak with four mountain ranges, deserts, and a coast rich in crags and cliffs. Beta has suffered tectonic stress and is mineral rich. It is also the location of the Great Shinar Forest. Gamma is the largest continent, has the highest rainfall, and in the centre is a most disagreeable swamp with distasteful fauna and flora and nine slow rivers that cross savannahs with plenty of predators and prey. Delta has beautiful landscapes; Songerl Bay is perhaps the most beautiful part of Delta.

There are four spaceports.

Station A is near Ascensor on Alpha. Pharisee city is also on Alpha.

Station B is on Beta, with Cambria Town to the west and the Great Shinar Forest to the east, along with the Lilank Prairie. The prairie runs all the way to the Aeolian Ocean, which separates Beta from Alpha. The Irfle Woods are in the middle of the prairie to the east of Station B. The Mystic Hills are to the west of Cambria town, and it is in these hills where you find the Great Mother Reef, which is the reason for the rare earth mine there.

Station C is on Gamma at the brink of the Great Gorge at Felker's Landing. The Arcts, an ancient human race, inhabit the crags in the Gaspard fastnesses of Gamma.

Station D is on Delta near Sonc Town, beside Songerl Bay. The Sonc Saloon overlooks the bay.

The Great Gorge at Felker's Landing is five-hundred-feet wide and two-hundred-feet deep. The gorge is a swamp over which dense black ferns grow; there is a net of walkways above it from which one harvests kikinuts from the ferns. The river Amer flows through the town into the gorge; the three inns, the Prospero, the Black Tamber and the Fazirab are south of the river.

MARISH SQUARE KM 21

A square in **Sailmaker Beach** where the **Route Slideway** terminates.

MARKAB PL 27

Notorious for the unbridled confusion of architectural styles into which this system has slid. As an aside, it may be that the Master slipped and meant Marhab rather than Markab.

MARMONE NL 29

This is the world where there exists a class called the Sensenitza, or the People of Grace. In the High Season, people spend all their money on pleasures, costumed balls, festivals, and banquets. In the Low Season, they work, lie, cheat, and steal to earn money to pay for the High Season. One of the centres of the High Season is Piri-piri, a palace half in and half out of a garden.

MARMONFYRE GE 78

A world where people have snub noses and orange hair.

MARQUARI KM 37

Provincial capital of **Garreu**, province of **Scythia**.

MARSKENS BD 101

A place seen by Dwyddion as he rose in the Institute. Dwyddion? Remember him? Self-absorbed, trouble-making twonk. Typical of the Institute, they'd have the rest of us in the Stone Age, but they still travel on fine space-yachts and stay at the best hotels whilst trying to look as if they aren't enjoying it. Myself, I would have them nailed upside down to the doors of places of public entertainment for the edification of the masses. Need I say more?

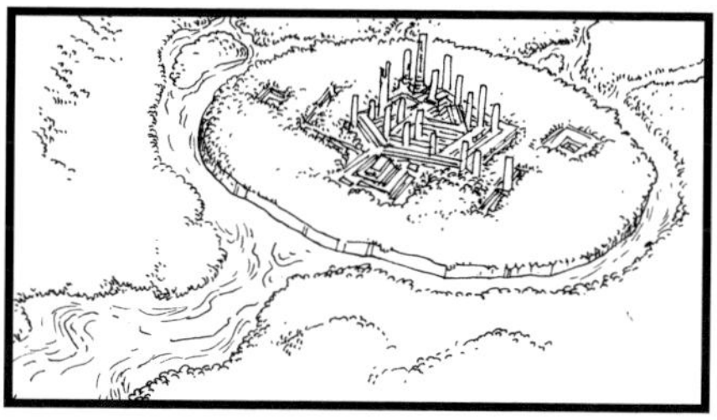

MARUNE MA 37

Alastor 933, it is almost on the "cold" edge of the Cluster in the Fontinella Wisp. It is a complicated system. Maddar (a red dwarf) and Cirse (a green star) swing close around each other. Furad, an orange dwarf, orbits close around Osmo, a blue dwarf, and Marune orbits Furad along with Haune and Douaune, both dead worlds. The two groups of stars rotate together around their common centre of gravity. Day and night are complex and there are nine different gradations recognised. Marune is a small dense world with no great population. Rugged, with polar tundras and not a great deal of open water, there are vast equatorial bogs and very little inhabitable land. **Port Mar** is the largest city. The Rhunes dwell in the Rhune Realms, east of Port Mar on the North Continent. The Rhune Realms are a succession of enormous mountain ranges, high crags, snow and glaciers, and the peaks stretch into the atmosphere above the snow line. There are a multitude of small rivers draining small valleys and forming small lakes.

Majartown, home of the original human settlers, the Majar, is falling into ruin. Most Majar live in the Old Town at Port Mar.

There are three scarps or sharp ridges which run to block the route between Port Mar and the Realms; after you have flown over them, in a desolation of rock and ridge is a small forested valley used by Port Mar as a prison — no guards are needed as one cannot walk out.

Various of the Realms are Scharrode, Gorgetto and Eccord; the first two are comparatively equal, Eccord has grown more powerful, Disbague is small and insignificant, and Torre is little better.

The "capital" of Scharrode is Benbuphar Strang, which is in an irregular valley fifteen miles long and up to four miles wide; at the eastern end, a cascade falls two thousand feet into a lake by the town of Esch.

Dwan Jar (the Whispering Ridge) separates Eccord from Scharrode; the Tassenberg separates Gorgetto from Scharrode.

The principle village of Eccord is Elde; four rivers have been diverted to create a circular waterway, with Belrod Strang on an island in the middle.

MASCARENE F 174

The home world of Mascarene Rum. A word of advice: whilst you might consider adding hot water and a lump of brown sugar, please don't let anyone use this to make pepper rum.

MASKE MT 1

One of the double planets, Maske and **Skay**, which orbit the star **Mora** in the Great Hole. Colonised long ago, the population has diverged from the human norm to become Homo mora, as opposed to Homo gaea.

MAUDLEY SPACE STATION SK 54

Contains a penal colony considered reasonable by those sent there, less bad than the **Frogtown Pits**.

MAUDLY WASTE BD 184

From "The Avatar's Apprentice" in *Scroll From The Ninth Dimension*.

MAUDWELL'S STAR PoC 54

Leo JN-44. The chief world of this star is **Dimmick**.

MAUNDY RIVER STATION BD 191

One of the stations on **Bethune Preserve**.

MAZ GE 3, 87, 95

A planet circling the white dwarf sun Khis, with a large frigid moon (Oloë). An ancient world, with half a dozen shallow seas and a few ranges of low hills separated by swamps or undulating plains with sluggish rivers.

Axistil is on a low plateau somewhat north of the equator. For tourists there is plenty to see.

The Great Kykh-Kych Swamp is about a thousand miles north of Axistil. Kanitze, a ruined Gomaz castle and tourist lodge, is north of the swamp. There is an Ubaikh castle in the same area, near the Black Cliff Inn resort, separated from Kzyk territory by the Shimkish Mountains and the Steppe of Long Bones. It is forty miles across the mountains from the Ubaikh castle to the Steppe of Long Bones.

In the southern hemisphere is the Andantinai Desert with the Great Cairn. There is also the Golgath Inn on the Plain of Skulls. Finally, for nature lovers, there are gargoyles in the Shimkish Mountains.

MAZDA T 58

A yellow star, halfway along **Mircea's Wisp**, it has four planets, three frozen rocks in outer orbit and the inner planet **Soum**.

MEAMONE BD 170

A magic star written of by Howard Alan Treesong. Make of it what you will; I couldn't possibly comment.

MEAUGHE BD 85

This river flows through Meaughe Vale, along the southern flanks of the **Skak Range**, on **Boniface**.

MECHANICS COAST PL 117

This is on **Lyonesse**.

MELBOURNE F 84

A city on **Earth**.

MELNOY HEIGHTS SK 146

A suburb of **Avente** above **Sailmaker Beach**.

MERGENTHALER KM 56

A small continent on **Krokinole**.

MERIONETH APARTMENTS SK 135

An apartment block in **Remo**, near **Avente**. The area is popular with **Sea Province University** administrative staff.

METHEL F 49

Third planet of **Cora**, **Argo Navis 961**; the sister planet to **Dar Sai**.

METHUEN GP 50

The star of **Koryphon**.

MIDAS MOUNTAINS PL 7

In upper **Phrygia**.

MIDOR MOUNTAINS BD 30

The mountains are renown for their cableways, but, alas, no one has seen fit to elucidate which world the mountains are on! One is supposed to see further if one stands on the shoulders of giants. Ha, if the giants are too tall, all you see is the inside of cloud.

MIEL PL 108

A star deep within the **Sirneste Cluster**.

MILDRED'S BLUE WORLD AS 322

A world occasionally visited by Floreste and the **Cadwal** Mummers.

MIRAMONTE BD 11

A hotel on **Avente**'s **Esplanade**.

MIRASSOU F 66

The moon of **Dar Sai**.

MIRCEA'S WISP
AS 11

A curl of up to ten thousand stars which streams away from the **Perseid Arm**.

MIREILLE
L 102

A white dwarf, the star of the planet **Star Home**.

MIRIOTES
F 174

The world on which you will find **Farewell Station**.

MIRKY POROD
EOE 25, 153

On **Earth**, it is in Draczeny. It is a castle in the Moholc not far from **Kiev**, at the head of a steep forested valley near Lake Jerest, under the shadow of the Carnat Mountains. The nearest village is Tzem on the River Sogor. The inn is the Iron Pig. For tourists who wish to get there from one of the major spaceports, take the subterranean slideway to Anthelm, then a feeder tube to Passau. From there it is airship to Draczeny and then omnibus to the door of the Iron Pig. As an aside, at Draczeny you can also catch a plane for Zagreb.

MIRSTEN
L 169

A world with a single inhabited continent dominated by a central mountain massif, the coasts covered with forest. Timber is the main export. The starport is Falziel. The city is less than a mile a side; within the city each building has the same specifications, differing only in size, all with a glossy red-brown dome surmounted by a slender finial. The old port city of Skolpnes was destroyed by a flood, and Falziel is the replacement. Taverns are marked by Atlas, carrying Old **Earth** on his shoulders, and, if you are looking for somewhere with decent ale, the Court of King Gambrinus is recommended.

MISK
KM 96

The land beyond the mountains on **Thamber**.

MIZAR SIX
SK 104

Home of the Tunkers, a religious sect whose men and women wear identical clothes, shave their heads, use a language of 812 words and eat identical meals at identical times.

MIZAR'S THIRD
SK 94, F 84

The planet Gersen was thought to come from. The Mizar system is near **Caph IV**.

MOLANDER ABBEY
BD 184

From "The Avatar's Apprentice" in *Scroll From The Ninth Dimension*.

MONA
BD 83

One of the inner planets of **Vega**, a cinder of scorched stone.

MONTROY
L 182

The world on which you will find Bantry's Bog and the Institute of Transcendental Metaphysics. An interesting combination that tells you pretty much all you need to know about the nature of humanity, the universe and life.

MORA
MT 1

A star at the very centre of the **Great Hole** with two planets, **Maske** and **Skay**. The two planets rotate around each other as they both rotate around their sun. Both worlds are inhabited and have been for years without measure.

MORBIHAN
NL 164

A world in the back region of Aquila where bandits are a problem.

MORGAN MOUNTAINS
KM 37

They form the border of **Garreu** Province of **Scythia**.

MORLOCK
L 41

A world in **Argo Navis**. Some patrician families live overlooking Faurency Weald, with the countryside spread all the way to Leyland Forest.

MORNEY'S TOOTH BD 94

A peak on one of the ridges in the **Pritz** badlands, **Boniface**.

MOSS ALRUNE F 176

House for sale in **Llalarkno** for a million SVU.

MOSSAMBEY AS 13

This world exports furniture and panels of semi-precious stone.

MOUDERVELT BD 109, 118

The sole populated planet of **Van Kaathe's Star**, slightly larger than **Earth**, with a single continent sprawling two thirds of the way around the equator. An old world with wide prairies and meandering rivers. The colonists divided it into 1,562 separate realms, or Lands, which are pretty much independent.

MOULDER L 136

An orange star with twenty-two planets among them. There is one inhabited world, **Blenkinsop**.

MOULTON'S WORLD AS 189

The home world of **Virgo Junction** where a dozen different liners call.

MOUNTAIN WILDS KM 47

On the world of **Image**. Given that it is a place where satin-green skin-tone, embroidered jackets and ruffled gaiters are currently fashionable, perhaps the Mountain Wilds set the sartorial tone for the rest of the planet.

MOUNT PLEASANT SK 161

A settlement in **Ferrier's Cluster** whose entire population was enslaved by the Demon Princes.

MOY VALLEY F 7

A beauty spot in Llinliffet's Land on **Aloysius**.

MURCHISON PL 32

A single planet smaller than **Earth** with one continent; the main export is tapestries.

MURCHISON'S STAR PL 20, 32

The base of Gascoyne the Wholesaler who deals in slaves (amongst other things). It is thirty light years beyond the **Pale**.

MYRA BD 101

A town in **Trans-Iskana** on **Alphanor**.

MYRDAL F 36

On **Boniface**, the site of the Interworld Court.

MYRMIDON? BD 19

The source of Myrmidense porcelains? Yes, I'm guessing.

MYSTERY GROTTO KM 37

On **Earth**'s moon, it houses an incomprehensible mechanism. (It probably boots up in MS-DOS.)

NAHARIUS PoC 42, L 194

A world in Virgo GGP 922, the population tends to concentrate in Trajence, near the spaceport. Just east of Trajence is an extinct volcano down which flow three streams, which seep through wooded glades and mix with springs; the waters are claimed to have healing and regenerative properties. Let us admit it, trade has been bad; there are only so many people out there who are both gullible enough and rich enough to be lured to Naharius to take the waters. Hence the articles in the popular press about "the Exxil pool" and the mythical world of **Kodaira**.

NAHUTTY
BD 84

Another of the few little towns on **Boniface**.

NAIDNAW SHADE
F 48

One of the older, rougher shades on **Dar Sai**.

NATRICE
AS 286

This is one of the worlds on the usual circuit of the **Cadwal** Mummers, who tend to visit dull worlds. The planet is roughly symmetrical, with a narrow equatorial sea (the Mirling), bounded by coastal plains that both to the north and south become temperate uplands, mountains and frozen tundra on the poles.

In the north, the area beyond the coastal plain is known as the Lanklands, in the south, the Wild Counties.

Most cities are on the Mirling. Halcyon City (the second city), Poinciana (the spaceport and largest city), and Summer City are the more festive areas; Lanklands is rather dour and dull.

For tourists I would suggest that Mirlview House is a hotel that achieves intolerable results with minimal effort; the Rolinda is modern and cosmopolitan.

NEAPOLIS
PL 47

A city on Europe.

NEROLI
GE 155

On this world the Barking Desert is known for its windstorms.

NEUSTER OCEAN
KM 99

Ocean on world of **Lorgan**.

NEW CALVARY
AS 322

A world occasionally visited by Floreste and the **Cadwal** Mummers.

NEW CONCEPT
BD 15

There is a space terminal five miles from the city of **Starport** on New Concept, which is a planet with three moons circling **Marhab Six**.

NEW GORCHERUM
BD 102

A planet where the "Peas and Beaners" are an influence. Need I mention that Dwyddion is involved?

NEW HOPE
SK 155

A world in the **Beyond**.

NEW OSSINING
SK 63

The third largest city on **Olliphane**, on the shores of **Lake Clare**.

NEW WEXFORD
SK 160 | PL 28

A city on **Aloysius**, home of the Elucidarian Press. It is a major financial centre with banks and brokerage houses in the city centre and the shops and dwellings in old houses set on twisted streets on the hills around.

NEW WEXFORD SPACEPORT
F 51

The spaceport serving **New Wexford**. It displays the stunning originality of bankers in everything but creating ever more convoluted ways of charging you for the privilege of being allowed to play with your money.

NICHAE
KM 45

This is a small spaceport on the shore of the **Calopsid Sea** where one lands to catch the airship for **Sul Arsam** and then **Interchange**.

NIGHT LAMP
NL 220

This star is on the extreme edge of the galaxy, even further out than Yellow Rose. It is a vagabond star that has broken free of galactic gravity and wanders alone.

NILO-MAY

NL 209, 215

Single planet of the sun Yellow Rose, chief spaceport Loorie. East of Loorie are the Hoo-Woo Hills, to the west across ten miles of morass is the Bay of Bismold, to the south and north are farms and other enterprises and further out a few outback stations. The rest of the planet is uninhabited by humans. An equatorial desert circles the planet with occasional channels connecting shallow oceans to the north and south. Oily rivers rise in the desert uplands and flow through forests and swamps.

Loorie boasts a number of commercial enterprises including the Fragrant Hotel, the Peurifoy Refreshment Parlor, the Bon Ton Salon and a Fifth Grade IPCC office. As an aside you will probably get a better cup of tea in the IPCC office than in the Peurifoy Refreshment Parlor.

NION

EOE 257, 272

Circles the sun **Pharisse**, a medium-large planet of 1.03 g and with a thirty-seven hour day. There are nineteen moons; the most obvious are Lilimel, Garuun, Seis, Zosmei, Maltasar, Yanaz, Sigil, Ninka, and Shan. Much of the food is derived from pold, which is derived from suspensions of pollen blown onto lakes and seas and then set in layers that can be up to yards thick. The main city and spaceport is Tanjaree. For the tourist there are the rock workers of Eladre who have carved their city from a mountain; the Shadow-men who live around the Plain of Standing Stones and who will become murderers during certain lunar phases; and Gangrils who transform pold into strange substances, most of them mind altering or capable of wreaking havoc with the human body chemistry; plus clans of vagabond jesters. For sane folk there is always the spaceport for a ship out.

There are twenty hotels in Tanjaree, but, of those fit for discerning off-worlders, I will list in order the Cansaspara, the Superbo, the Haz Warrior, and the Novial. Shun the others unless you have learned to love pold.

As for other sights, there is the Tangting Forest where one of the autochthonous monsters models his fellows in clay for his own recreation and our horror.

The other cities are Sirmegosto, six thousand miles south and east of Tanjaree, Tyl Toc, four thousand miles due west, plus half a dozen isolated towns, among them, Hooktown near the Tangting Forest, Moonway on the Plain of Standing Stones, Whipple's Camp under the Scintic Crag, Port Klank and the romantically named but immediately forgettable Yellow Blossom.

The Plain of Standing Stones stands with William Schulz Buttes to the north and the Gerhart Pastels to the south. The main purpose of visiting is to loot the graves of the Shadow-men, a dangerous but occasionally lucrative profession.

NOAILLE

BD 83

One of the inner planets of **Vega**, a cinder of scorched stone, holds one face steady to Vega, and is notable because of the rains of liquid mercury which fall on the dark side, flow to the hot side where they vaporise and return to the dark side.

NOUMEA

F 84

A place on **Earth**.

NOVA BACTRIA
BD 48

Known only as the world of origin of Sharrod Yest, a murder victim.

NOVAL
SK 51

A planet in **Rigel Concourse**, it orbits **Vega**.

NOWHERE
SK 55 | PL 52

A planet of the **Rigel Concourse**. The home of Lenka workmanship; these are panels intricately inlaid with wood, bone and shell.

NUMENES
MA 7 | WA 5

This world is the residence of the Connatic and is the capital of the **Alastor Cluster**. When approaching Numenes, ships pass by Blazon, which orbits outside Numenes, where the Whelm has a navel base and inspects all incoming ships.

The central spaceport is at Commarice, three miles in diameter. There are no real continents, just islands; virtually everyone owns a boat. The Connatic's Hospital is on the island of Flor Solana. From there, to get to the Connatic's Palace, take an air-cab across Flor Solana to Moniscq, a town on the sea, then under the Ocean of Equatorial Storms by a submarine tunnel to Tremone Island. From there an air-bus takes you south to the palace (known as Lusz), which is a tower standing on five pylons, standing on five islands. The lower three decks are reserved for tourists who can stay remarkably cheaply; then come the government departments and the offices of the Twenty-Four Agents, then the Ring of Worlds and up to the College of Anthropological Sciences. The Connatic has a suite at the pinnacle which rises ten thousand feet above the sea.

NUMOY
PoC 198

The Klutes come from the Bleary Hills on the world of Numoy. In Enders Valley there are several institutions for lost children, the largest is the Enders Valley Foundling Farm.

OAKLAND
BD 30

Where ever it is, it has boulevards. And you ask me, do I care any longer?

OCEAN ISLAND
AS 138

Off the east coast of **Deucas** on **Cadwal**, a relatively popular place for romantic picnics.

OCK LAKE
KM 62

Near the Card River Estuary on **Krokinole**, it doubtless sees romantic picnickers.

OIKUMENE
SK 16

That part of occupied space in which the rule of law can be said to run.

OLAM
SK 186

The probably mythical home of the probably mythical jewels of Olam.

THE OLANDER
F 79

A hotel in **Serjeuz** catering entirely for **Darsh**.

OLANJE
GP 8

At the foot of Panorama Mountain, the city of Olanje on Szintarre, **Koryphon**, is effectively the capital of the planet; it is certainly the spaceport. It is also the home of the Mull, the organ of government for the whole planet of Koryphon.

Many of the inhabitants have villas in the Carnelian mountains.

OLDENWOOD
F 175

Home of Adario Chanseth in **Llalarkno**.

OLD HOME AND PRAIRIE LANDS
BD 101

A place seen by Dwyddion as he rose in the Institute.

OLD LUMAS
AS 322

A world occasionally visited by Floreste and the **Cadwal** Mummers.

OLD MARKET
PoC 40

In **Salou Sain**, one can find a theatre of the nude, a dog-barber, shops selling exotic herbs and vegetarian pellets, plus the Club Kit-Kat, a cellar cabaret.

OLD SOCCO
BD 9

The old market in Tangiers on **Earth**, it may once have been known as the Grand Socco.

OLLIPHANE
SK 63 | PL 27

The densest of the planets of the **Rigel Concourse**, it is highly mineralised with vast hydro-electric potential and has become the most highly industrialised world of the Concourse. This is shown by the inordinately large amounts of concrete that tend to be used in virtually any construction.

OPHIUCHUS
NL 9

A large constellation on the celestial equator.

ORPO
SK 51

A world circling **Pi Cassiopeia**.

ORVIL
T 136

A place way out at the edge of the Reach.

OTT'S RESORT
BD 140

Out on **Skooney's Lake**, where comparatively wealthy people visiting **Gladbetook** would tend to stay, out of town rather than having to mix with relatives in town.

PADRAIC
BD 83

One of the inner planets of **Vega**, a cinder of scorched stone.

PAGHORN
NL 208

A world in the Aries sector, Phasis is the space terminal. Cray is a backland village, hard by the Long Bog, where at night men and women who fancy adventure go out wearing masks.

PAING
PL 5

The spaceport and town of Godoland, **Sarkovy**.

THE PALE
PL 111

"The invisible barrier theoretically separating order from Chaos, the boundary between the **Oikumene** and **Beyond**." Note that this barrier is not fixed and slowly and inexorably moves outwards as the Oikumene develops. Yet historians have commented that this has merely served to dilute the Oikumene rather than eliminate the Beyond. In some of the Master's works, it is obvious that the Oikumene is now the totality of human space, yet this does not mean that the outer fringes are any less lawless.

PALLAS
BD 48

Home of the Pallas Technical Institute, on **Alcyone**.

PALMETTO ISLANDS
SK 116

A popular retirement destination on **Ys**.

PAMATRA VALLEY
WA 53

The Pamatra Valley is an example of the rich farm lands on the scarps which separate the Weirdlands from **Arrabus**. The inhabitants of Arrabus will sometimes summon up the energy to forage there; they have no money to buy food, their tokens are worthless, and the only real trade they can offer is sex for food.

PAMFILE
KM 132

A town on the continent of **Zaccaré** on the world of **Quantique** where scents are of immense importance.

PARAGUAY
EOE 200

On **Earth**. For the tourist, to see the back waters of the Southern American continent, go to Alonso Saavedra on the Rio Tanagra; from there you can take a sky coach to Biriguassu, then south and west across the Pampas to the mining town of Nambucara (where the Stella d'Oro Hotel serves fine steak in large portions). The air-bus from there goes to Aquique (best hotel, Universo) and then to Lago Angelina in the southeast. From Aquique there is a bus to Pombareales (where one can stay at the Hotel Monopole). If you think this is remote, travel on the same road for another thirty miles, turn left at the back of beyond, and you come to Salgas. In Pombareales they will assure you that persons born in Salgas are as common as dirt.

PARILIA
SK 44

A city on **Pilgham**?

PARIS
PL 47 | BD 30

A city in Europe, it still has boulevards.

PARNASSIO
F 176

The house of the Zames in **Llalarkno**.

PATRIS
KM 56, 63

The Whitelock capital on **Krokinole**, it sprawls for miles along the Card River Estuary and onto **Ock Lake**. The Old Quarter has houses a thousand years old; upriver is New Town around the great River Arches. Between the two is a dingy industrial area.

PEDDER-DULAH
BD 101

Home of the Polders, a place seen by Dwyddion as he rose in the Institute. Busy little beaver, our Dwyddion, don't you think? Interfering busybody.

PENWIPERS HOTEL
BD 30

A good hotel in **Pontefract** on Old Tara Square. The hotel is very old fashioned, but comfortable, and guests will find they have appropriate clothing laid out for them. If you can afford it, stay there; highly recommended.

PERGOLA REGION
PoC 102

The region in which the world of **Kyril** is situated.

PERSEID ARM
AS 11

Part of the constellation of Perseus.

PERSIMMON LAKE
BD 199

Near **Gladbetook**, **Moudervelt**.

PFITZ
PoC 215

The sun of **Mariah** (more properly Laura Ardelia Pfitz).

PHARISSE
EOE 258

A yellow-white star, the sun of **Nion**.

PHARODE
SK 39

Again I merely comment that an author paid by the word will not leave an entry blank purely because the Master somehow neglected to mention what or where Pharode was.

PHI OPHIUCHI
SK 59

The home star of the world **Sarkovy**.

PHRUSTER'S INN
F 6

An ancient inn at the foot of the Dunveary Crags. On Llinliffet's Land on **Aloysius**.

PHRUSTER'S PROSPECT
F 6

Near the inn this is a well-known viewpoint allowing the tourist to look out over **Lake Feamish**, **Rath Eileann**, and vaporous **Moy Valley**. On Llinliffet's Land on **Aloysius**. A trail leads up from Ffolliot Gardens to the Prospect. Do not attempt it unless reasonably fit or, of course, going down rather than up.

PHRYGIA SK 56

One of the seven nearly contiguous continents on **Alphanor**.

PI CASSIOPEIA SK 51

A star in the **Rigel Concourse**.

PILGHAM SK 44

A planet in the **Rigel Concourse**.

PLAISE NL 43

In a local swarm not far from the edge of the galaxy. One can stay at Sern in the foothills of the Kindred Mountains; nearby is Pol Pond where the mountain folk go for their ablution rite after they sing in Kouhou Chasm.

POISON INN PL 11

The main tourist hotel in **Paing**, on the world of **Sarkovy**.

POLDOOLIE BD 85

A small town, largely inhabited by Fojos (a variant of humanity) on the banks of the river **Meaughe** on **Boniface**.

POLWHEEL BAY BD 198

Port Wheary, **Aloysius**, is on this bay.

PONTEFRACT KM 22 | BD 12

A city on **Aloysius**, notable for its incessant mist. An important publishing and financial centre. The heart of the oldest section of town is St. Paidrigh Square.

PONTEFRACT SPACEPORT F 51

The spaceport serving **Pontefract**.

POORLEG'S RIVER BD 94

This river rises near Mount Lucasta and flows down through the **Skak Range** to join the **Meaughe**, **Boniface**.

PORVING F 200

From "The Avatar's Apprentice" in *Scroll From The Ninth Dimension*.

PRIMARCHIC WA 44

The extent of humanity is divided into four areas, the **Alastor Cluster**, the Gaean Reach, the **Erdic Realms** and the Primarchic. The Primarchic is best described as an aggregation of stars rather smaller than the Alastor Cluster. It has at times been controlled by a Primarch but currently has reverted to its default state of war, factionalism and chronic disorder. One of the major roles of the Whelm is that it provides protection against raids from the Primarchic.

HOTEL PRINCE FRANZ LUDWIG PL 67

The most elegant rendezvous of **Rolingshaven**.

THE PRITZ BD 94

A peak on a ridge of the same name in the **Skak Range**, **Boniface**, across **Airy Gulch** from **Voymont**.

PROTAGNE AS 322

A world occasionally visited by Floreste and the **Cadwal** Mummers.

THE PURPLE ROSE SYSTEM AS 11

On the edge of **Mircea's Wisp**, this system is composed of three stars; Lorca, a white dwarf, and Sing, a red giant, swing close together around each other, whilst this double star is orbited by **Syrene**, a yellow-white star of ordinary size and luminosity.

QUANTIQUE SK 51

The great estate houses of the **Oikumene** maintain two thirds of all locator ships, and there are only a few sophisticated worlds on which the estate houses congregate, among them **Alphanor**, **Cuthbert**, **Boniface**, **Aloysius**, **Noval**, **Copus** and **Orpo** (the last two orbiting **Pi Cassiopeia**), Old **Earth**, and, of course, Quantique. A planet where the natives, even day labourers, have an aloof air.

QUININE SK 55

A planet of the **Rigel Concourse**, the sixth planet of **Alphard the Lonely**.

QULI-QUN
BD 19

A source of rugs. Unfortunately, their marketing, whilst good on stressing the quality and durability of the product, seems somehow to have neglected such trivial details as to location of the supplier.

RAPUNZEL HOTEL
SK 65

A hotel above a subway exchange near **Kindune** Spaceport on **Olliphane**.

RARATONGA
SK 55

A planet of the **Rigel Concourse**.

RATH EILEANN
F 6, 12

It is a city founded by the Ambrosians, on Llinliffet's Land on **Aloysius**, also a spaceport. Describing the city in detail, it is divided, right to left, into Ffolliot Gardens, Bethamy, Old Town, the Orangery, with the **Domus** behind. Then **Estremont** on a **Lake Feamish** islet. These are the cross of the T; the stem straggles north for miles, through Moynal, then Drury, **Wigaltown**, Dundivy, Gara with its Dulcidrome, and finally Slayhack with the spaceport.

REDEMPTION PARK
F 175

The park lies between **Twanish** and **Llalarkno**.

REIS
F 21

Sixth planet of **Gamma Eridani**.

REMBRANDT HOTEL
PL 48

On the Hoeblingasse in **Ambeules**; frankly I think you'd be foolish to stay anywhere else, especially if you are claiming expenses.

REMO
SK 91

A small town on the **Ard Hook** near **Avente** and the site of the **Sea Province University**. A charming enough place, but never visit it during term time.

RHAMNOTIS
TA 26

Alastor 965, a world where the culture has been planned to benefit the health and pleasure of the inhabitants; the original settlers resolved to put aside the filth, discord, and waste of normal society. Poverty is unknown; the work week is ten hours, which, although grinding unremitting toil for a bureaucrat, is easy enough on the ordinary citizen who then spends time in preparing the fetes, carnivals and fantasies which bring in the tourists. The original settlers came from **Triskelion**. A cult called Tamarchô has a history of wanton violence and degradation and was concentrated on Silver Mountain before being eliminated by the Whelm.

RHEA
T 85

The planet Rhea has a canted orbit, a backward rotation and an asymmetrical shape, and is not so much a planet as the result of a juncture of numerous large asteroids and fragments of a dead star. It is mined extensively. There are two main continents, Wreke and **Myrdal**, separated by the equator and the Straits of Scaime. Wreke is where the mines are, with the city of Tenwy being the residential area of the continent; Myrdal is to the south and is reserved for the estates of the Twelve Families who bought the mining rights. The Scaime at places is only forty miles wide, but the tides and currents which join the two oceans can reach thirty knots. It was decided to bridge the Scaime; the bridge is at Tenwy, as is the spaceport. From the terminus, one passes through a manufacturing district into an administrative district, uniform blocks of glass and concrete faced with black opal veneer.

The hills behind are residential, with orderly streets of grey houses with pink roofs, but with arcades, colonnades, bulbous domes and at least two, and perhaps six, pencil-cypress trees; Silurian Circus is near the end of the bridge. On the coast of Wreke is the village of **Yipton**, where Yip workers have taken wives from local women.

RHEAS

BD 190

A continent on **Bethune Preserve**.

RIGEL CONCOURSE

SK 54 | KM 37

The Concourse consists of twenty-six planets, most of them not merely inhabitable but salubrious. Discovered by **Sir Julian** Hove but named by the clerk Roger **Pilgham** from the **Maudley Space Station**.

ROBERT PALMER'S STAR

NL 9

Towards the far edge of the **Cornu Sector** of **Ophiuchus**, Robert Palmer's Star is a brilliant white star with a dozen planets; only **Camberwell** is inhabited.

ROCK-WALLOWS

BD 129

North of the **Junifer River** boglands on **Moudervelt**.

ROLINGSHAVEN

PL 47

A large city on the west coast of Europe divided by two rivers, the **Gaas** and the Sluicht, and by the Evres Canal. In the north is Zummer, grim district of apartment towers and malls, but on the Heybau, a promontory hooking out into the sea, is the Handelhal Conservatory, the Galactic Zoo and the Kindergarten. South of the Sluicht is the Old City, a confusion of small shops, inns, hostels, offices, beer caverns and book stalls dating back to the Middle Ages. Here is the fish market along the Evres Canal overlooked by the university. **Ambeules** is across the canal, a district of nine hills covered with homes, and with wharves, warehouses, shipyards and mudflats from which Flamande oysters are taken. Across the Gaas from **Ambeules** is Dourrai, an area of small houses with a lot of industry and fabrication plants along the shore and southward.

ROSALIA

AS 39 | T 91, 95, 105, 120

A rather rough and ready little world to the back of the Pegasus Rectangle. There are eight large continents, myriad islands and occasionally a body of open water large enough to pass for an ocean.

The continents are Ottilie, Eclin, Koulou, Yellow Nelly, La Mar, Trinky, Hortense and Almyra.

Port Mona, on Eclin, is the largest town, between twenty thousand and forty thousand inhabitants, depending on transient workers. There are a number of hotels, agencies, shops, offices of the double government (the Factor's Association, which represents the ranchers, and the Board of Civil Regulation, which governs the rest of the populace; neither recognises the other), plus a spaceport.

North of Port Mona are two tourist hotels, the Multiflor and the Darsovie Inn, both five storeys high and elegant, but there is also Whipsnade House, a rambling irregular structure, which is also a hotel.

The ranches are large. Boggins' Willow Glen covers almost a million square miles;

Aigle-Mort and Stronsi Ranches are about the same; Black Lily and Iron Triangle only about one hundred thousand square miles; Flalique about sixty thousand. For the tourist there are the Wild Honey Plains with flowering plants and moths disguised as flowers, Dinton Forest where the trees are up to seven-hundred-feet tall, the Mystic Isles of Muran Bay and the multi-coloured desert known as Tif.

Shadow Valley Ranch includes the Morczy Mountains, Pavan Lake and a dozen smaller ponds, several fine forests and parkland savannah.

It may be near here one finds the **Garden of Dido** where Calyactus, Oomphaw of the Yips, mysteriously died. Lipwillow, on the banks of Big Muddy River, is the principle town and spaceport for those doing business with the nearby Shadow Valley Ranch, and there is the Big Muddy Hotel for tradesmen and toursits. A bar, Poolie's Place, is at the landward end of the pier which stretches fifty yards out into the river.

The Yips originally indentured to work at Honeyflower Ranch have absconded to create a settlement near Tooneytown on Ottilie; the Stronsi Yips have decamped to a settlement they have formed at the Mystic Islands, the Shadow Valley Yips have moved to near Lipwillow, and the Baramond Yips live in grass shanties just past the spaceport near Faney's Marsh.

Of further interest to tourists, in Tooneytown on Ottilie there is the Old Divan Hotel. While travelling by flier, it is well worth taking the trip to the Stronsi Ranch headquarters beside the Fesque River. You fly northeast of Port Mona then over the Saraband Straits, then Koukou, Almyra and onwards over the Maenadic Ocean, until you come near Port Twang; this is a small town. Thirty miles north is the Stronsi Ranch headquarters.

Bainsey Castle is the site of the old house on the coast of the Maenadic Ocean and is being developed as a tourist hotel.

ROTTERDAM SK 36

An old city on **Earth** with footpads in its back alleys.

THE ROUTE SLIDEWAY KM 21

Runs north, paralleling the **Esplanade**, then curves through the **LoSasso Tunnel** to terminate at **Marish Square** in **Sailmaker Beach**.

ROYAL OAK HOTEL PL 44

A good **London** hotel, a block off the Strand.

RUDYER MOOR F 16

An area of bleak upland in the Mournan Mountains near **Rath Eileann**; the site of the battle of the First Vegan Wars.

RUPH SHADE F 129

In **Dar Sai**, it is on the edge of Terwig Waste, on the route from **Serjeuz** to **Dinkelstown**.

SABIK KM 30

Alternative name of the star **Eta Ophiuchi**.

SABRA PL 32

The city on **Murchison**, home of tapestry production. It is on the shore of the north polar sea centred around Orban Circus, a volcanic stub.

SADABRA F 19

A place where Lens Larque owned a house with a large semi-circular room. In this he ate his favourite foods (great heaps of hork and pummigum) whilst casually flogging his enemies, manacled naked to rings on the wall. For want of better suggestion, it might well be that the house is on **Dar Sai**.

SADAL SUUD FOUR F 8

An inhabited planet.

SAFRONILLA NL 215

A planet so far **Beyond** that even five thousand years later it has never been rediscovered. Wilbur Wailey kidnapped many beautiful women and populated the planet with them, and his children by them.

SAGBAD
KM 98

The nearest trade centre to **Interchange**.

THE SAHARA SEA
PL 82

On **Earth**, it is not clear from the writings of the Master whether the sea wholly or partially displaces the desert, but, given that Timbuctoo still stands, it is probably the latter.

SAILMAKER BEACH
SK 93

A district north of **Avente**.

ST. CRODECKER'S CONTINENT
BD 85

One of the continents of **Boniface**, at the centre of which is the area known as "World's Moil."

ST. DIARMID'S INN
BD 41

A large cosmopolitan hotel in the heart of **Pontefract**.

ST. KILDA'S BAY
BD 198

On the coast north of **Port Wheary**, **Aloysius**.

ST. STEPHEN
KM 119

City on **Boniface**, the home of the publication *Pancretic Review*. Which goes to prove that even on Boniface literacy is not entirely dead. Although the cynical might point out that the journal survives through off-planet sales.

SAIRLE CITY
BD 140

On **Copus**, home of Mama Potts's Swillery where pepper rum is served.

SALMI SWAMP
BD 217

An area of swamp near **Blue Forest Camp**, **Bethune Preserve**.

SALOU SAIN
PoC 11

On **Vermazen**, Salou Sain is across the continent from **Lilling**, the home of the College of Definable Excellences at the Varley Institute. There are fine houses on Dingle Terrace, of which one is Sarbiter House.

SANCELADE
EOE 104

A city on Old **Earth**, destroyed in the Alienate Convulsion and rebuilt to the specifications of the autocrat Tybalt Pimm. The Kyprian Quarter was designated for light industry, etc., but is now a resort of artists and vagabonds; it's surrounded by bistros and small shops for the purchase of oddments. A good hotel is the Marsac, at the edge of the prestigious Gouldenerie, close to the Kyprian Quarter on the banks of the River Taing. For a prestigious business address, think about renting in Flavion House, which is on Alixtre Square on the oppose side of the Gouldenerie. Clarmond at the western edge of Sancelade houses Gohoon Galleries.

SANDUSK
KM 22

The inhabitants of this world are known as Sanduskers; they pride themselves on facing forward rather than looking back, and keep few memos or souvenirs of the past. In the Gaean Reach, they are best known for their cooking; small enclaves of Sanduskers are made to live downwind of others, ideally where the wind will blow the smell out over the sea.

SAN FRANCISCO
F 84

A city on **Earth** which is apparently still there; so much for all this talk of earthquakes.

SANGWY SHADE
F 123

An isolated settlement on the Sheol Barrens of **Dar Sai** inhabited largely by ruffians and criminals. This being said, an unbiased observer might feel called upon to comment that, with such a population, it is only the geography that differentiates if from any other shade on the planet.

SANKLAND
KM 56

A large continent of **Krokinole**; North State has the "Hole through the World" that the tourists marvel at.

SAN-SEVERE L 50

A world on which is found the spaceport of Lorca and Aetna University.

SANSONTIANA SK 50

A city of **Braichis**, one of the nineteen independent nations on **Olliphane**. The city is the second largest on Olliphane and is home of the Feritse Precision Instruments Company.

SARBANE PoC 155

A place of legend? On a par with Old **Earth** in the imaginations of many who have never left their home village, never mind their home planet.

SARDANIPOLIS KM 51

The home planet of the Sardanipolitans, surely. (I am sorry, but even I am embarrassed by that. But when the Master fails us, what can I do?)

SARKOVY SK59 | PL 5

The single planet of **Phi Ophiuchi**, a dim world of steppes, swamps, black forests and morasses. The planet almost redefines the word flat; one steppe runs into another, with perhaps a forest thrown in to break the monotony. The inhabitants are notorious for their development and use of poisons, all of which they make from natural substances from the world around them. Isn't nature wonderful?

SASANI KM 44

The home of **Interchange**, it is also known as Aquila GB 1201 IV in the Star Directory.

SAUDAL SUUD F 188

This might be same place as Sadal Suud; if not, the Master left us nothing to remember it by.

SCORPIO KM 65

This is one of the constellations into which the **Oikumene** is divided.

SCROPUS PoC 108, 114

This world circles **Tacton's Star**; it is the fourth planet, six thousand miles in diameter, with a dense core and standard gravity. There are three continents, two polar, one, Ayra, equatorial; on this is the main town and spaceport Duhail. Nearby is the Refunctionary.

SCYTHIA SK 56

One of the seven nearly contiguous continents on **Alphanor**, the most sparsely populated and probably the most bucolic.

SEA PROVINCE UNIVERSITY SK 77

At **Avente**, **Alphanor**.

SERAFIM L 42

A town in the **Beyond**, not too far from **Dusa**.

SERCEY GE 29

Geison Weirie from Sercey had hired Gomaz from **Maz** as shock troops to take Sercey. Thus sparking a major war and the Triarchic jurisdiction.

SERJEUZ F 53

A major settlement on **Dar Sai**, the spaceport consists of a rectangle marked out in white where they expect people to land; it is the only facility of such sophistication on **Dar Sai**.

SERLE KM 120

A city on **Quantique**, it is the home of the publication *El Orchide*.

SESSET BD 184

From "The Avatar's Apprentice" in *Scroll From The Ninth Dimension*.

SFERINDE SELECT
F 79

A hotel at **Serjeuz** catering for Methlen only; the service is rumoured by some to be no more than adequate.

SHADE
F 74

On **Dar Sai**, shades are enormous parasols up to five hundred feet high and covering up to twenty or thirty acres. Water is pumped from aquifers up onto the top surface, down which it runs to trickle down in sheets, veils and cool mists. The **Darsh** live under the shades.

SHADIM ROAD
BD 200

From "The Avatar's Apprentice" in *Scroll From The Ninth Dimension.*

THE SHAGGETH
BD 94

One of the ridges in the **Pritz** badlands, **Boniface**.

SHANARO SEA
BD 82

On **Cytherea Tempestre**, it washes around **Wild Isle**.

SHANITRA
F 73

The largest chunk of the dead star known as **Fideske**, which currently orbits **Methel**.

SWAMPS OF SHARMANT
F 21

Swamps on **Hyaspis**, fifth planet of **Fritz's Star**.

SHILLAWY
EOE 79, 85

On **Earth**, it is the home of the Library of Ancient Archives.

SIGIL 92
L 42

A planet with an IPCC post at the town of Olfane.

SIKKIM
PL 92

On **Earth**, it is a source of precious rugs traded throughout the Reach.

SINGHAL ISLAND
SK 115

An island on **Ys**.

SINKIANG
PL 82

A resort area on **Earth**.

SIN-SAN'S TAVERN
SK 28

A tavern in **Brinktown**. Provided you remember that the clientele are, or have been, by profession extortionists, blackmailers, pimps, murderers, arsonists and the like, they are good enough company. One is warned against letting your tongue run away with you after a couple of drinks, as most of these men are willing to come out of retirement when presented with a suitable financial opportunity, even if it is merely selling your story to one of the Demon Princes.

SIRENE
SK 108

Not too far from **Mizar Six**, where men wear masks from birth to death.

SIRIUS
KM 112

The Dog Star.

SIR JULIAN
SK 55

In the **Rigel Concourse** "an eccentric, tumbling, odd-shaped fragment of chondritic pumice."

SIRNESTE CLUSTER
PL 108

The cluster is in **Aquarius Sector**.

SIRSSE
BD 69

Source of the tincture "Liquor of Life."

SISTER PLANETS
GE 172

Traditionally know by this collective name, they are **Wittenmond**, **Gietersmond**, and **Skalkemond**, which circle **Jingkens Star**.

SKAKER CITY
PL 5

The capital of the Skakers.

SKAKERLAND
KM 56

A continent of **Krokinole**, the land was settled by a schismatic cult of the Skakers who went to **Olliphane**. Of interest to tourists, the undersea forest is off the coast of Iksemand, Skakerland.

SKAK RANGE
BD 85

This mountain range runs diagonally across World's Moil on **St. Crodecker's continent**, **Boniface**.

SKALKEMOND
GE 183

The third of the **Sister Planets**, it specialises in banking, maths, cosmology, music theory and critical evaluation.

SKANSEL SHADE
F 89

A "suburb" of **Serjeuz**, one of the shades that make up the settlement.

SKAR SAKAU
KM 114

A mountain range, the homeland of fierce barbarians on **Thamber**, amongst whom are the Tadousko-Oi.

SKAVA STEPPE
KM 114

The home of Skodolak nomads on **Thamber**.

SKAY
MT 1

One of the double planets, **Maske** and Skay, which orbit the star **Mora** in the **Great Hole**. Colonised long ago, the population had diverged from the human norm to become Homo mora, as opposed to Homo gaea.

SKOHUNE TOWER
F 179

An office block in **Twanish**, **Methel**.

SKOONEY'S LAKE
BD 140

Not far from **Gladbetook**, **Moudervelt**.

SKOUSE
KM 9

Skouse is the main town on **Bissom's End**.

SLAYHACK SPACEPORT
F 51

The spaceport in the Slayhack suburb of **Rath Eileann**.

SLAYMAN
BD 84

Yet another of the few little towns on **Boniface**.

SLAYMARKET ISLE
BD 173

Mentioned by Howard Alan Treesong as the home of the Moals, whatever he meant by that.

SMADE'S PLANET
SK 9

A small stony world in the middle **Beyond**. Whilst discovered earlier, it was not exploited until 1479 when Smade settled there. It is the sole planet of **Smade's Star**, and the native flora consists of lichen, moss, primitive vines and palodendron, with some pelagic algae, whose presence gives the sea a black tint. The fauna consists of simple protozoa and a few white worms and gelatinous creatures.

SMADE'S STAR
SK 8

A white dwarf star in a relatively empty region of space.

SMADE'S TAVERN
SK 9

Situated on a shelf of heath between the Smade Mountains and the Smade Ocean, and set precisely on the planet's equator is Smade's Tavern. A long two-storeyed structure with a high gable, a double row of windows along the front and rear and chimneys at either end. It sits in about three acres of ground surrounded by a whitewashed stone fence and is the only inhabitation on the planet. Smade also exercises control over two sheltered valleys; in one he grows fodder for the livestock and vegetables, in the other graze a small herd of cattle and a small flock of poultry. There is also a landing field marked out further along the shelf of heath, within comfortable walking distance of the tavern.

His beer, Smade's Own, is sold in bars across the galaxy.

SOGDIAN PL 108

The fifth planet of **Miel**, with an hourglass continent on which is the city of **Atar**.

SOGMERE PL 20

A place on **Sarkovy** about which nothing else is known. It is unlikely to be wholesome.

SOMEWHERE SK 55

A planet of the **Rigel Concourse**.

SOUM AS 19, 286 | T 58

Half way along **Mircea's Wisp**, circling the yellow star **Mazda**. It has four near identical continents, around one world ocean.

It is the financial and commercial centre of **Mircea's Wisp**. A world on which there is a pilchard cannery, it is one of the worlds on the usual circuit of the **Cadwal** Mummers, which tend to visit dull worlds. It is an old world, mountains worn down; innumerable rivers wander into the seven seas that have only lackadaisical storms.

SOUMJIANA AS 189, 352 | T 60

On the world of **Soum**; the city is also the spaceport. In the centre of the city is the Octacle, a great eight-sided plaza, overlooked by the Travelers Inn. For those just looking round, there is a semi-industrial suburb, Urcedes; the Gastronomical Institute by the lake; then the wide Boulevard of Acclaimanders, which has a row of monumental black iron statues on either side, each representing a long dead grandee; the Tydor Baunt University; and Pars Pancrator Plaza, on which sits the Bank of Soumjiana. From the plaza one walks down the Promenade of Strong Women to the cab-rank. Interestingly Soumjiana takes Yips from **Cadwal** who have been indentured for penal reasons. They serve for a couple of years and are then free, but can never return to Cadwal. No one is quite sure whether they manage to get any work out of them or not.

SPICA SIX BD 23

The home world of **Virgo Junction** where a dozen different liners call.

STANISLAS F 167

It was from this planet, more specifically from amongst the members of the exclusive club of the Aretioi based in **Zangelberg**, that the planet of **Methel** was colonised.

STAR HOME L 101

The second planet of **Mireille**, a small dense world with a breathable atmosphere and Earth normal gravity. The climate is congenial. The northern continent is under permanent ice; the other continent tends to be a steppe of waist-high grass with a few low hills. The inhabitants wander the coast; the sole spaceport (a few old warehouses) is at Palactus in the centre of the steppe. Miskitter Marsh, Blackwater Camp, and Sluiceway Riverside are places where the local semi-nomadic inhabitants occasionally congregate.

At Torqual Downs, there is a repository of the rugs produced by the population, much sought after by persons of good taste.

STARPORT BD 18

A city on **New Concept**, it is five miles from the space terminal where the spaceships actually land.

STAR-WANDERER'S INN F 195

A Bar (the capital B is well deserved) specialising in the working men's trade in **Twanish**, and one I'd recommend. It carries guest beers from all across the Reach, and the local brew, Hangry's White Ale, is good enough to stand comparison, even in that company. An elderly woman plays the euphonium with gusto and decision, which makes up for any lack of repertoire.

STOCKHOLM SK 131

On **Earth** it is known for its regal functions.

STROMA
AS 15

Originally intended as guest houses for society members doing research work, Stroma on **Cadwal** is a town of tall narrow houses, black or dark umber, with doors and window trim painted red, white and blue, built on eight levels with majestic views of the fjord. One favoured inn is the Iron Barnacle which is built on an offshore crag. Another is the Utward Inn. The Spaceman's Rest near the air terminal is considered Stroma's second tavern.

STRYLVANIA
SK 131

Known for its lawn fetes (and damn all else apparently).

SUL ARSAM
KM 45

A station in the **Da'ar-Rizm** desert where the air-ship connects with the surface car route to **Interchange**, twenty miles away.

SUNNYRAIN HIGHLANDS
F 174

On **Krokinole**, known for coffee production.

SUSIMARA ISLANDS
BD 48

The source of Lily Milk, a precious ceramic ware, on the **Yellow Sun Planet**.

SVENGAY
F 84

On **Caph IV**, a lively little world.

SWANIBEL RIVER
BD 131

Joins the **Sweet Trelawney River** near **Gladbetook**, **Moudervelt**.

PORT SWAVEN
BD 84

The initial landing and processing place for convicts arriving on **Boniface**.

SWECHER'S INN
BD 139

The inn in **Gladbetook**, **Moudervelt**.

SWEET TRELAWNEY RIVER
BD 126

Gladbetook, **Moudervelt**, is on the banks of this river.

SYLVANUS
EOE 286

A world somewhere in Virgo, Kyper City is on it.

SYRENE
AS 11

One of the three stars of the Purple Rose System in **Mircea's Wisp**, Syrene has three planets; only **Cadwal** is inhabited.

TACTON'S STAR
PoC 102

The sun of the planet **Scropus**.

TAMAR
GE 3

A planet in the Nova Celeste Sector. The Fabrilankus Café in Twisselbane is reasonably priced for travellers. The town also has the Pleasure Gardens, a central market, and a pageant where young women dance and pose with not too many clothes. To enter the Pleasure Gardens with too much money is as foolish as to enter with too little.

TANAQUIL
BD 189

Space field and capital / entry point for **Bethune Preserve**.

TANCRED
EOE 71

The home of the Tancred firefox, known for its "danger tendrils."

TANGIERS
BD 9

A city of **Earth**.

PORT TANJEE
PoC 69, 77

The space port and capital of the world **Taubry**, an orderly place, where everything is kept just so. Fimrod Lane connects the Rambler's Rest to the plaza. From the plaza (where miscreants hang in cages) one walks sixty-two yards up Melcher Lane to the Owlswyck Inn.

TANQUIL
GP 18

A world, otherwise unknown, which has at least one good young ladies' finishing school.

TANTAMOUNT
SK 55

A planet of the **Rigel Concourse** renown for its shipyards.

TARN
PL 43

The site of the West Europe spaceport.

HOTEL TARQUIN
PL 123

A splendid hotel in **Avente**, **Alphanor**, although some may hint that it is overpriced for what you get.

TASSADERO
AS 286, 359, 363

This is one of the worlds on the usual circuit of the **Cadwal** Mummers; the circuit tends to visit dull worlds. The world orbits **Zonk's Star**. Fexelburg is the spaceport.

Three races share the planet: the Zubenites of Lutwiler Country, numbering perhaps one hundred thousand, then there are perhaps fifty thousand nomads on the Great Steppes and far regions, and a further three million inhabitants of Fexel Country around Fexelburg.

A useful hotel in Fexelburg is the Lambervoilles; the Nouveau Cri Salon across the way will provide appropriate dress for their clients. But avoid Flinders Inn; it is where the nomads stay.

If travelling to Pogan's Point Seminary (a favourite of treasure hunters) in Lutwiler Country, which is out on the eastern steppe, it is normal to break the journey at Flicken where there is a bus depot and food can be arranged.

TATTENBARTH
BD 172

Mentioned by Howard Alan Treesong as a home of nymphs. I pass no comment.

TAUBE
KM 37

A drowsy sun-struck village on the shores of **Jermin Bay**, in the province of **Garreu**, on **Alphanor**.

TAUBRY
PoC 67, 74

A world circling the sun **Vianjeli**. The world has three continents. Farst and Wints are left to savage natural fauna; Liro is inhabited but divided into thirteen cantons of rich diversity. The three main cities are **Port Tanjee**, Melanchrino, and Semmerin.

TAU GEMINI
SK 43

A star system.

TEEHALT'S WORLD
SK 18

A planet of great beauty discovered by the locator Teehalt, its day length is twice that of **Earth** standard. The trees dominate the planet; open areas are grassy with occasional rare clumps of flowers. The dryads are bipedal and to human eyes look like a form of walking tree.

There are also winged hawk-like creatures which will attack the dryads.

TEMPLE OF ORGANIC UNITY
BD 25

On the planet of **New Concept**, the Temple of Organic Unity is a building between the space terminal and spaceport built for the original settlers. The settlers were vegetarians who lived on alfalfa sprouts, collard greens and bits of native vegetation. They evolved into barely sentient herbivores, and the temple decayed into a classical ruin.

TERCE

PoC 122, 137

The planet that orbits the star, **Bran**. Dulcie Diver is the main space port and there is an IPCC presence that renders the immediate environs comparatively safe for tourists.

It is a world of moderate size with one continent, which almost encompasses the world, leaving a single narrow ocean and a lot of small seas and inlets. There are few rivers, a lot of timber, and a large swamp on the west coast. Ferocious beasts prowl large areas. There are two mutually hostile peoples, the Shuja and the Meluli, whose economic survival depends upon taking, tanning and selling human skins. Whilst Shuja will tend to hunt Meluli for skins and vice versa, neither party objects to surreptitiously killing tourists who wander off alone. There is a secondary spaceport at Sholo where one can buy beautifully tanned human skins. Panton Scarp stretches above Sholo spaceport. Mel is a village of the Meluli at the top of the scarp; the Shuja live at the foot of the scarp. For travellers the Glad Song Tavern is almost safe.

TERENCE DOWLING'S WORLD

T 162

Smuggler's City is there.

TERRANOVA

BD 41

A region of the world **Denebola V**.

TEXAHOMA

KM 56

An area on **Earth**, where riots occurred within living memory.

TEX WYNDHAM'S PLANET

T 79

The home of the short-tailed lizards; nothing else needs to be said.

THAERY

MT 2

The area on Thaery settled by Credential Renunciators from **Diosophede**. They divided the area into twelve districts, one for each ship, and set out to become a bucolic people, dedicated to the natural environment and natural substances, pledged to duty, simplicity, and respect for status. They would make themselves the exact opposite of the Diosofids of Diosophede from whom they had split.

The individual districts can be seen on the map and will be mentioned only when something of interest is within them.

For the tourist it should be noted that the inns of Thaery, by law, are situated no more than seven miles apart and are uniformly pleasant, clean and comfortable, inspected by Bureau of Trade inspectors to ensure this happy state of affairs continues.

THAMBER

KM 13

This planet is at the extremity of **Beyond**, a place of legend, remembered by the verse

Set a course from the old Dog Star
A point to the north of Achernar;
Fare until, on the starboard beam,
Six red suns toward a blue sun stream
Sleight your ship to where afar
A cluster hangs like a scimitar.
Under the hilt to the very extreme
And dead ahead shines Thamber's gleam.

Thamber is at the very edge of the galaxy. It was settled immeasurably long ago and was then forgotten and slipped back into barbarism from which it is barely emerged. **Despaz** is the only continent to boast civilised life. **Gentilly** on the western shore of Despaz is perhaps the most civilised; to the east of Gentilly is **Vadrus** and, beyond that, the land of Mirk. Save for a few feuding cities and principalities scattered along the east coast, the rest of the continent, indeed the rest of the planet, is home to barbarian tribes. Between **Misk** and Vadrus there is usually war, with

Gentilly siding with Vadrus.

This level of civilisation is comparatively new; it is barely two hundred years since Tyler Trumble conquered Vadrus and built the city of **Carrai**, whilst about the same time Jadask Dousko found Misk a land of herdsmen, with **Aglabat** a fishing village.

THE HALLS SK 133

A night spot in **Avente** near **Les Sirenes**.

THEOBALD STATION BD 110

In the **Land of Lelander** on **Moudervelt**; it has a spaceport.

THESSE GE 151, 165

A planet. The main city is Cassander with the Hotel of the Worlds and the Caelzie Empire Inn. Junis is a suburb of Cassander. Further out are the Trembling Mountains at the foot of which is the Trembling Waters Academy. The Academy is on Tanjaree Cove.

Keen sailors among you might like to sail across the Florient to the Hesperids, or through the Shadow Islands. One could keep a ketch at Port Sant and sail through the Mirage Islands to Tinghal and, if the trade winds held, to Geraniol.

THRAW F 201

From "The Avatar's Apprentice" in *Scroll From The Ninth Dimension*.

THROY AS 12 | T 178

A continent of **Cadwal**, Throy stretches from under the polar ice into the southern temperate zone; it specialises in dramatic typography with crags, chasms, and towering cliffs. **Stroma**, above Stroma Fjord, is inhabited. At Throop's Heath the andorils play their odd version of bowls, whilst on Cape Wale, the great southerly storms dash against the cliffs.

THRUMP F 10

The spaceport/city for **David Alexander's Planet**.

THUMBNAIL GULCH SK 172

The hideout of Dasce on the surface of an unnamed red dwarf.

THURBEN ISLAND AS 287

It is off the east coast of **Deucas** on **Cadwal**. A roughly circular mound of sand and volcanic debris, two miles in diameter, covered with grey-green thornbush, some thyme trees, and some semaphore dendrons. There is a crag of basalt in the middle and a lagoon two hundred yards wide. Do not swim in the lagoon under any circumstances.

TINTLE'S SHADE F 25

A public house on Pilkamp Road, **Wigaltown**, **Rath Eileann**, which is patronised by members of the small **Darsh** colony. The nearest omnibus stop is Noonan's Alley, should you be interesting in visiting.

TOWER OF LONDON SK 26

On **Earth**, in **London**, where coronations take place.

TRANQUE EOE 122

This world orbits Bellatrix V and is renown as the home of quasi-living crystals.

TRANS-ISKANA BD 101

The southern continent of **Alphanor**.

TRASNOY NL 212

The spaceport for Trasnoy is Port Hedwig, the world is comparatively close to **Nilo-May**.

TRAVELER'S INN F 79

A decent hotel in **Serjeuz** catering for anyone.

TRIARCHIC JURISDICTION GE 11

The great space "empires" come together at the world of **Maz**, where the Gaeans, the Liss and the Olefract allied to crush the Gomaz. They all maintain sectors in the town of **Axistil**.

In the centre of the town, both the plaza and the building of the **Triskelion** are under the combined jurisdiction of all three powers, the Triarchic jurisdiction. Frankly, each power is terrified of the other two arming the Gomaz and using them to destroy the balance of power. Equally frankly, arming the Gomaz would be an act of suicidal lunacy for anyone.

HOTEL TRICERATOPS BD 189

A tourist inn at **Tanaquil** on **Bethune Preserve**.

TRIESTE EOE 176

On **Earth**. For tourists wishing to visit, it is reached by subterranean slideway. Trieste Central Depot is ten miles south of the old Trieste station. To help you get your bearings, Via Malthus is on the western bank of the Canal Bartolo Seppi in the Porto Vecchio district. Hotel Sirenuse in the old city is recommended. One enters the Plaza Dalmatio by way of the Via Condottiere and then out onto the Via Strada. The Via Severin crosses the Canal Flacco by the Ponte Fidelius into the Porto Vecchio, all wharves and narrow canals. The Way of the Ten Pantologues runs beside the Bartolo Seppi Canal, full of bistros, shops selling coins, autographs, dead stars, cakes and model spaceships.

TRISKELION TA 17

The original home world of the settlers of **Rhamnotis**.

TROVENEI PL 7

In **Phrygia**.

TRULLION TA 13, 32

Alastor 2262. The lone planet of a white star on a spray of stars curling out toward the Cluster's edge. A small world, mostly water with one narrow equatorial continent, Merlank. Hundreds of rivers run down from the central mountains, creating rich agricultural land and a bucolic population not prone to strive overmuch. There are four spaceports, Port Kerubian on the north coast, Port Maheul (in Staveny Prefecture) on the south coast, Port Gaw on the west coast and Vayamenda in the east. A hundred miles east of Port Maheul is the market town of **Welgen**.

Circanie is a pleasant mountain town; one can get an air-bus there from Welgen, and a surface car will take tourists to the scenic Vale of Xian. It is narrow, the hills on either side steep, the river flows quietly. The Trevanyi (a gypsy/nomad people) bury their lesser dead here and their more important dead deeper within the valley.

TSAMBARA MA 52

Alastor 1317. Here you can get connections from the central Cluster out along Fontinella Wisp.

TWANISH F 49

Spaceport and first city on **Methel**, it is predominantly inhabited by about fifty thousand "Mongrels," or wanderers, who provide services to the Methlen, and a large colony of **Darsh** who do the menial tasks.

TWAST'S PLACE BD 149

On **Krokinole** , it is by repute one of the most intolerably drunken dens in the **Oikumene**.

TYR GOG
T 81

Pegasus KE58. It has nine planets, six are small balls of rock, one is a gas giant, one a ball of ammoniacal ice, and the last, the planet **Rhea**, has a dozen anomalies.

TYRHOON
T 127

A world on which is found the Mocar Sea. It may exist, but it was mentioned only by Namour, which guarantees nothing.

TSARGRAD
PL 47

A city in Europe.

UMBRIA
SK 56

One of the seven nearly contiguous continents on **Alphanor**.

UNICORN
SK 55

A planet of the **Rigel Concourse**.

URSA MINOR
EOE 98

A region of space.

USHANT
NL 130, 166

A world congenial for human settlement with no noxious fauna. Where the River Leis joined the River Ling, there is a vast flooded plain of innumerable small islands on which the settlers built their individual airy palaces. This became Dimplewater, city of a thousand bridges. Travel from Ushant spaceport to Dimplewater is by train through a flamboyant jungle known as the Gages of Lyrhidion.

VADILOV
KM 30

Planet circling **Eta Ophiuchi**.

VADRUS
KM 113

A principality on **Thamber**.

VALE
PL 118

Also known as Virgo 912 VII. Home of the Druids.

VALHALLA
SK 44 | PL 120

A planet in the **Tau Gemini** system known as Tau Gemini VI.

VALISANDE
SK 55

A planet of the **Rigel Concourse**.

VANELLO
KM 65

A resort world to the back of **Scorpio**.

VAN KAATHE'S STAR
BD 109

A star with one planet, **Moudervelt**.

VARSILLA
GE 81

The world of nine blue oceans and ten thousand sea peaks and eleven million islands (and twelve billion sand flies, and sixteen billion glass nettles and twenty billion tourist villas), Meyness is the central capital. Palestria on Jailand is beautiful and placid.

VASCONCELLES
BD 101

A place where Dwyddion was resident Thwarterman as he rose in the Institute. I believe the planet is still civilised, and the populace has managed to avoid sliding into subsistence serfdom.

VASSELONA
F 21

A continent on the planet **Reis** (sixth planet of **Gamma Eridani**).

VEGA
SK 43, 51 | F 5

One of the stars that make up the **Rigel Concourse**.

VERLAREN
F 21

Second planet to **Komred**, **Epsilon Sagittae**.

VERMAZEN
PoC 11

A pleasant world on which **Salou Sain** is situated.

VIANJELI
PoC 67

Sun of the world **Taubry**.

VIRE
F 8

A city of **Sadal Suud Four** where ships may be registered.

VIRGO AXX-1 THIRTEEN
NL 259

Calley's Junction is on this world. From here you can get ships to most of the back sector.

VIRGO JUNCTION
BD 23

On **Spica Six**, where a dozen different liners call.

VOYMONT
BD 94

A ridge near **Athmore Violet** in the **Skak Range**, **Boniface**.

WABBER'S FOUNTAIN
F 77

One of the major settlements of **Dar Sai**.

WAKWANA ISLANDS
KM 30

On **Quantique**.

WALPURGIS
SK 55

A planet of the **Rigel Concourse**.

WAMBS COUNTY
BD 52

A district near **Pontefract** where one would find persons of good taste, impeccable breeding, modest wealth, and quiet respectability.

Doubtless they still break wind in the bath.

RIVER WANN
AS 19

A river that flows through **Araminta Station**, feeding the lagoon behind Clattuc House.

WARRAM FOREST
F 202

From "The Avatar's Apprentice" in *Scroll From The Ninth Dimension*.

WAYVODE
F 201

From "The Avatar's Apprentice" in *Scroll From The Ninth Dimension*.

WELGEN
TA 14

A market town a hundred miles east of Port Maheul or **Trullion**. It is famous for its hussade stadium (the largest in the prefecture) and is the market town for "**the Fens**."

WELLAS
MT 2, 174

On **Maske**, it is the home of the Waels, who were descendants of the fourteenth colony ship which crashed (or was shot down) after theological differences became ideological. It is almost opposite Cape Junchion in **Glentlin**. Erdstone Pool is the normal harbour of destination. It is entered via a channel called the Ballows with no mole, so ships only enter on the turning of the tide. The village is along the shore beside the boatyards; visitors are recommended the Tanglefoot Tavern. Note well, the toddy has a life of its own.

Two days journey inland is a place called Durruree where there is Zul Erdour; their place of judgement in the trees.

WEST EUROPE SPACEPORT
PL 43

One of the major space ports of **Earth**, at **Tarn**. Connected to **London** by tube.

PORT WHEARY
BD 197

Down the coast from **Pontefract**.

WIEN
PL 47

City on Europe.

WIGALTOWN
F 25

A suburb of **Rath Eileann**, a coarse and dismal neighbourhood with a dozen or more off-world enclaves.

WIGGAL RIVER
BD 110

A river flowing through the **Land of Maunish**, **Moudervelt**.

WIGGS' WISP
NL 105

The boundary to a remote region of space.

WILD ISLE
BD 41, 52

On **Cytherea Tempestre**, "it is a kind of dreamland, not altogether real," known for casinos and gambling. In short it is a tourist resort.

WIRFIL

BD 101

A world where the Institute led a campaign against pesticides.

WITTENMOND

GE 172

One of the three **Sister Planets**. Wittenmond, **Gietersmond**, and **Skalkemond** circle **Jingkens Star** along with three other worlds. Wittenmond has set up a thriving mercantile system. Diestl is a city of considerable charm built on the hills surrounding Mount Flouderklaf on the banks of the Lemon River near the Irruptor Ocean. Diestl has a spaceport and the Traveler's Hotel; there are seventy-three purlieus (almost suburbs), each with its own set of characteristics.

WYSROD

MT 3, 20

On **Maske**, Wysrod is the largest town on **Thaery**, virtually a city. It lies on Duskerl Bay in the district of Famet.

It is a sober city, with irregular narrow-fronted buildings, all different. The Marine Parade runs along the bay; the other main streets, all tree lined, meet at Travan Square, which is the centre of government. On one side is the Parloury, which has three bureaus, the Landmoote which represents the middle and lower castes, the Convention of Ilks, which represents the great families, and the Five Servants.

A harbour has been created by joining the Cham, which is the wooded spur that forms one side of the bay, to Point Sul on the mainland by a mole and two tide locks.

For the unpretentious looking for decent accommodation and decent food, the Sea-Wrack Inn is to be recommended. Similarly the Jiraldra is a fashionable pavilion on Marine Parade.

WYST

WA 5, 150

Alastor 1716. The sole planet of the white star, **Dwan**. The planet has two continents, Trembal and Tremora, which can best be regarded as forming an hourglass shape separated by the one-hundred-mile wide Salaman Sea. From the north to south, or, as the locals say, from the Northern Gulf to the Moaning Ocean in the south, the "hourglass" is about four thousand miles tall.

The Salaman Sea littoral, a strip stretching no more than twenty miles inland, is the land of **Arrabus** which is the major inhabited area. To the south are the cities of Uncibal and Serce, to the north the cities of Propunce and Waunisse, but the entire littoral is effectively one metropolis. Beyond the littoral, once one has climbed the flanking scarps, one enters the Weirdlands, which were once civilised but have been abandoned to forest. The southern edge of the hourglass, an area known as Blale, is not as cold as expected; it is warmed by an equatorial current, and folk live there in the town of Balad, where one can stay at the Old Groar Tavern. Balad is separated from the Weirdlands by Lake Neman.

The Weirdlands are inhabited by "witches" who are deaf-mutes by hysterical obsession.

There are two island continents, Zumer and Pombal, on the other side of the planet; they combine mountain crags and half-frozen swamps with a virtually nominal population.

XION

SK 44

A planet in the **Rigel Concourse**; it has a Northern Territory.

XI PUPPIS X
SK 120 | KM 37

This planet is notable for "Monument Cliff," which was carved by the Hexadelts or some other pre-human folk.

YAPHET
T 73

The planet circles **Gilbert's Green Star**. The flora is marsh-pod, algae, scruff (a bamboo-like shrub) — and dull. The commercial capital is Zaster; commercial travellers stay in tidy hostels decorated in psychologically correct colours, and, like the rest of the population, they eat healthy and nutritious food. The Excelsis Tower is on Boulevard Nine; there is no public transport — everyone jogs everywhere — but there are invalid wagons for the infirm. The Old King Tut restaurant is opposite the Excelsis Tower, but you might want to run to the Old Common, which is four miles along the Way of the Underwood.

THE YAR
F 200

From "The Avatar's Apprentice" in *Scroll From The Ninth Dimension.*

YELLOW SUN PLANET
BD 48

Home of Lily Milk, the precious ceramic.

YEO
BD 84

A city on **Aloysius**, relatively cosmopolitan.

YIPTON
AS 14

This town is the largest population concentration on **Lutwen Atoll**. With a population entirely of Yips, the only road to economic viability is to turn Yipton into a tourist resort. The Arkady Inn is built entirely of bamboo poles and palm fronds, the Pussycat Palace is famous throughout **Mircea's Wisp** for the affable versatility of the attendants. In Yipton nothing is free. The Hybel Canal flows through the town. And frankly, the whole place stinks.

YMMYR MARSH
F 200

From "The Avatar's Apprentice" in *Scroll From The Ninth Dimension.*

YS
SK 55

A planet of the **Rigel Concourse**, one notable foible of the population is they allow brother-sister marriage.

YSSINGES
EOE 25

A residence near the village of Tierens, which is fifty miles south of **Shillawy** on **Earth**.

ZACARANDA
SK 55

A planet of the **Rigel Concourse**.

ZACCARÉ
KM 132

The same name describes both an area and a people on **Quantique**. They are fixated with perfumes and scents.

ZAMBOANGA
BD 140

Remembered by most for the Lascar Quarter and the white curry. I would have thought many would have had happier memories of the chemist who sold them the kaolin and morphine afterwards.

ZAMSKI'S BOHEMIAN GRILL
PoC 41

On **Floiry Place**, in **Salou Sain** on the banks of the river **Chaim**.

ZANGELBERG
F 167

On the world of **Stanislas**, the site of the exclusive club of the Aretioi. The club itself is not what it was; some have contacts with **Methel**, others have financial holdings on **Dar Sai**, but the wealth or standard of living of those who remained on Stanislas is not to compare with those who emigrated.

ZANGWILL REEF

MT 1

This trailing band of stars marks the eastern extremity of the **Great Hole**. It has a baleful reputation, and I shall not trouble the dreams of the young by going into too many details.

ZECK

WA 20

Alastor 503.It circles the star, Mur; it is a world of one hundred thousand islands scattered across a hundred seas, the sole continent so covered with waterways as to be almost a collection of islands itself. Many families live on houseboats, and carved mooring posts are something of a local affectation. The Institute of Molecular Design is at Frayness. One of the prettiest areas is thought by some to be the Shard Sea.

ZONE STATION

PL 47

The sub-Channel tube station at **Rolingshaven**.

ZONK'S STAR

AS 311

Named after the pirate Zab Zonk, the world **Tassadero** circles this star.

THE GAEAN REACH, A MISCELLANEA

Whilst there has been a gallant attempt made to ensure that the gazetteer is definitive, a more casual, almost negligent attitude pertained in other departments. Still, I have made of their pathetic scribblings what I can.

CURRENCIES

Here we see the impact of history and population displacement.

First we see the **SVU** or Standard Value Unit. This was a universal currency in its day, backed by the major banks of the Oikumene. Ironically, because of its financial probity,* the SVU was happily accepted Beyond. The value of the SVU was, in theory at least, based on one hour of unskilled labour under standard conditions. Such a utilitarian currency seems to have lost favour and was largely replaced by the **sol**. This process seems to have been complete by the time the Beyond was finally absorbed into the Oikumene. The sol was somewhat more valuable, perhaps twice the value of the SVU. In some areas, the sol was replaced by a local

* Apparently bankers were known for their sobriety, lack of imagination, and a total disinterest in ingenious financial instruments as a source of short-term gains. Thus the criminal classes were forced to resort to the traditional enterprises of theft and extortion, unable to branch out into investment banking and derivative manipulation.

currency; hence, in Alastor Cluster, we know, they adopted the **ozol**. The ozol seems to have been virtually identical to the sol in value, with three-and-a-half ozols a day being the wage for low paid manual work or the producing of planetary gazetteers.

Note that whilst the SVU (for example) was normally seen in the form of notes,* many planets produce coins. Hence, on Boniface, the **three-piece** is worth three-quarters of an SVU.

* In some cultures the term "bills" is used, a bizarre practice but one which we confidently predict will diminish as educational standards rise.

SPACESHIPS

These range in scale from the small and often battered through to the vast and occasionally luxurious.

SPACE-YACHTS

At the bottom end of the range, you have the simple **air-boat**. These are often used as a ship's boat, convenient for collecting cargo when on planet or transferring passengers or materiel when one does not wish to trouble a spaceport with your presence or the authorities with the hassle of maintaining records of your presence and business. Some can operate outside the atmosphere.† If you don't wish to venture into the cold of space in something little larger than a family automobile and will restrict yourself to working within the atmosphere, you might consider a **sky-car**. These tend to be small three- or four-person flying vehicles. They are often used as utility vehicles.

Then we come to the **space-yacht** proper. We will start with the Fantamic Flitterwing. Not a commercial boat but a serviceable and competent space cruiser, with a small cargo hatch and accommodations for four. It has rivals; there is the Armintor Starship, which is less comfortable, and the Distis Pharaon, which is smaller.

In the middle ground, there are the Flecanpraun, the Sissle Wanderway, and the Scarab. The last is a more compact version of the Fortunatus Glitterway. Mention of the Glitterway brings us towards the top end of the market. The Clayhacker with its grandiose lines and fittings strives for this niche, but without success. Pride of place must go to the range of space-yachts produced by Fortunatus. Their aforementioned Glitterway series sets the standard against which others are measured. The basic Glitterway measures sixty-five feet from stem to stern. It has a large saloon, galley, three double cabins, storeroom, and utility room occupying the top deck. There is also a companionway leading three steps down to the control cupola. Below the top deck are the engine room, dynamics, crew's quarters, further storage, and utility rooms. A nice feature of the range is the exterior skin. A common colour scheme is enamelled white, with black delineators and dark red bands around the squat oversized sponsons, which, in the upper ranges of the Fortunatus line, were integral to the hull. The top end of the range can normally be picked up for about a million sols. The popular colour scheme is to have the hull enamelled a lustrous black with a trim of scarlet and mustard-ochre.

If you seek further luxury, then you are probably looking for the Golschwang 19 or the Sansevere Triumph. These typically cost over two million sols. Some of this can be accounted for by engineering excellence and having slightly more space, but most of the extra cost comes from the sheer luxury of the fittings.‡

† *But just because something can be done, doesn't mean it should be.*

‡ *Actually it is my opinion that the extra cost is accounted for mainly by the manufacturer's great profit margin.*

Finally for those who merely seek a workhorse, there is the Locator, Model 11-B, now produced by numerous builders and sold as Ariels, Cody Extensors, Spadway Hermits, and the like. They are broad-beamed craft of compact contour, all about fifty feet long, with only cosmetic differences from the rugged if spartan prototypes. Prices for such craft start at something over twenty thousand sols depending upon age, condition, and furbishments.

Those considering buying ought to beware of those boats listed as **space-cruisers**, such as the Glistmar Explorer Route space-cruiser. They're too small to be commercially viable working craft* and too large to berth with other yachts, meaning that you end up skulking amongst the more disreputable tramp cargo handlers and livestock carriers, which leads to one being mocked by one's peers.

LINERS AND BIGGER SHIPS

At the bottom end of the social spectrum are the cargo carriers and freighters. **Freighters** are normally larger and tend to cover long routes, which they traverse with remarkable regularity. **Cargo carriers** are smaller, erratic, and will carry anything, anywhere, for ready money.

* *By which we mean it isn't big enough to survive by shipping cargo and passengers, as opposed to charging them inordinately large amounts of money to travel to planets with looser morals or a more casual attitude to the use of recreational narcotics or sadomasochistic pleasures.*

That being said, for your ease, we include a list of ships and the lines that own them (where relevant). It was felt it might be useful for you to have some names to drop into the conversation. Note some companies call their ships **packets** rather than liners or freighters. A packet would be expected to be a little faster but to carry fewer passengers and more freight than the normal liner, and in less luxury. A **cargo-passenger** vessel carries more cargo than a liner and is slower and less luxurious than a packet.

Berenicia	A liner of the Black and Red Line
Distilcord	A rackety old freighter
Dylas Extranuator	A black, red, and gold space ship; probably a liner
Ectobant	A liner of the Prydania Line
Faerlith Winterflower	A Perseian Lines packet
Francil Ambar	A great passenger packet
Fratzengale	A reconditioned passenger transport
Gacy Wonder	A liner
Leucania	A liner
Lusimar	A liner of the Gaean Trunk Line
Lustspranger	A ship of the Demeter Line
Rondine	A cargo-passenger vessel
Sagittarian Ray	A liner. It has cabins, a promenade, dining salon with a pop-up screen giving the menu at each table and a great saloon
Samarthi Tone	A Green Star packet
Solares Oro	A cargo-passenger vessel
Sublume Overdyne	A Perseian Lines packet
Tristram Tantalux	A liner
The Wispen Argent	A liner

GENERAL TECHNOLOGY

SURVEILLANCE DEVICES

Let us start with the most innocuous.

The **call-button** is worn on the shoulder, normally by children and young teens; it seems to be a one-way radio allowing the parent to contact the child with instructions.

Beyond this we do not willingly go, if only because we may bring down on ourselves the attention of the Institute. But in the interests of clarity, we have a range of bugging and surveillance devices. The standard **bugging device** will have a near-invisible audio pickup, which will be attached (normally by wire but sometimes by wireless) to a recording device. It is normal to have the recording device attached to a telephone so you can interrogate it without having to re-enter the premises.

For surveillance there is the **stick-tight**. Throughout the galaxy there is a vast variety; we include five that are "popular" in more "civilised" areas.

- The servo-optical. This is a spy cell supported on rotary wings, remotely controlled by the operator.
- The automatic. A smaller cell, also on rotary wings, designed to follow a radioactive or monochromatic tag fixed to or smeared on a man or vehicle.
- The Culp spy-master. This is a semi-intelligent flying creature trained to follow any subject of interest; clever, cooperative, reliable, but relatively large and noticeable. Popular on some planets where a paranoid husband will hire one to follow their wife about. The wife gains the reassurance that her husband still cares, her reputation with her friends is boosted as they marvel that she is having an affair at her age, and the husband is reassured.
- The Manx spy-bird. A smaller less obtrusive creature, trained to perform similarly, less docile and intelligent, and more aggressive.

- The Manx spy-bird modification, similar to the above and equipped with control devices. If you are intending to use a Manx spy-bird, then, frankly, I suggest you spend the extra sols.

MATERIALS AND MEDICAL

Here we are at our most capricious. With a galaxy to explore, something regarded as normal on one world will be a novelty a few light years away, if they aren't connected by well-frequented space routes. Thus and so, an adhesive gel that can be smeared on two surfaces and doesn't "go off" until the surfaces are brought into contact is regarded as novel in some places.

With the simple commercial **hole-driver**, the operator merely has to touch the sleeve to a hard surface, stone, wood, metal, or synthesite and press the button, and a hole of exact dimension and depth is driven into the material. On a planet where every DIY enthusiast has one of these, what idiot equips his gendarmerie with powered armour?

As an aside, **synthesite** is a synthetic material on a par with stone, wood, or metal and has a very hard surface.

Talk of synthetic materials brings us to **marmelization**. When a body is marmelized, the fleshy tissue is replaced with a marble-like solid. On some worlds it is used to produce tombstones which are themselves the coffin and corpse.

Kits are issued as standard to travellers going to other planets, containing a mixture of substances to protect against various diseases, such as **rectification pills**. As with all these things, they are of variable efficacy; for example, most still contain Erythrist. This is useless, especially against Soumian itch.

This rather brings us on to medical. Genetic experiments banned in one place will be welcomed in another, but be warned by the tale of a geneticist from Alphanor who grew bored among the Zubenites and impregnated three dozen eggs with the sperm of racoons so the offspring grew tails. He also produced a thousand one-eyed creatures with one leg, blue spots, and enormous genital organs. Still, one cannot stop the progress of science.

An advance in medical science, the **neural probe** enables the expert to explore the mind and brain of the patient. Ideally, a pair of metal hemispheres clasps the patient's head, exposing only the nose, mouth, and chin, metal sleeves grip the patient's wrists and ankles, whilst metal bands immobilise the chest and hips.

When displayed on the screen, the brain is portrayed by a schematic chart showing bright yellow lines in a web.

The yellow lines represent overactive linkages; when they tangle into mats, they cause trouble. Some of the linkages may be as thin as spider webs, others may pulse with power. Sometimes the strands can become coiled and impacted into fibrous pads so dense that the individual nerve is lost. These tangles are a problem in that they are like black holes in the mind; nothing which touches these escapes.

In the hands of an intelligence service rather than a medical service, the investigation can take a different track. It is possible with care to tap into the various parts of the neural apparatus. The analytical process can then be set in motion and a particular episode in the patient's past can be explored in detail.

Nyaz-23 is a drug that facilitates deep hypnosis and is often used in combination with the neural probe.

In medicine, **pannax film** can be used to totally surround and sheath "Ogg's Plaque," an area of brain tissue, and cut it off from the rest of the brain. The results are obvious.

For those without the time or skill to use a neural probe and also lacking all ethical constraints, there is the **glockenspiel**. With this, a metal tube enters each of the victim's ears. It curves down through the sinal passages to emerge at the back of the mouth and out through the lips to form a horseshoe-shaped hook. The horseshoes are connected to the tympanum of the sound-bars. These will tinkle and jingle if the interrogator hits them with a silver wand. This apparently sends sound into the victim's brain. If you do it for long enough, the victim will probably confess to anything.

In an attempt to prove we are not barbarians, we offer up a mechanism for **refreshing with vapours**, used by some artists to provide a symphony of odours. The apparatus has a panel displaying knobs, toggles, bulbs, and other mechanisms. This panel controls hundreds of small vials. A selection from these vials is poured into a silver orifice, and a fan blows the scent to the audience whilst the artist prepares the next scent.

COMPUTING

For once, the Institute and I are at one. We march in lockstep. Who but a fool links computers together so that they may burble to each other in some electronic language faster than human thought? As for the results of such madness, they are three fold.

Firstly, the state and major corporations can accumulate vast amounts of data that they struggle to evaluate.

Secondly, it merely destroys the jobs of countless petty clerks, most of whom end up working for inspectorates where they do infinitely more damage.

Thirdly, it inevitably means that some pimply adolescent whose bowels would stutter were he* even to contemplate doing a day's work is thus enabled to bring down banks and embarrass his betters by drawing attention to their minions' moral infirmities. If the youth of today want pornography, they can, to put it crudely, grow a pair, go out, and buy it from the sort of sleazy emporium that deals in such materials. Thus I have spoken.

But there is still a considerable amount of use that may be made of computational devices. I will list and comment upon a few, as the mood is currently upon me.

The **communicator** is a desk-based system that can show pictures, data, and text, which travel down the telephone wires. It can also act as a **videophone**. One can interrogate the communicator, but one cannot add to its store of knowledge, save by accessing the central databanks.

A useful tool of the manager, the investigator, or the psychiatrist, the **computational device** produces a set of questions for the subject to answer. It monitors various biological tell-tales as it does this and thus produces an analogue of the subject's psyche. They are often linked to a **desk screen** so the operator can view the subject during the test without being observed.

* It normally is a he.

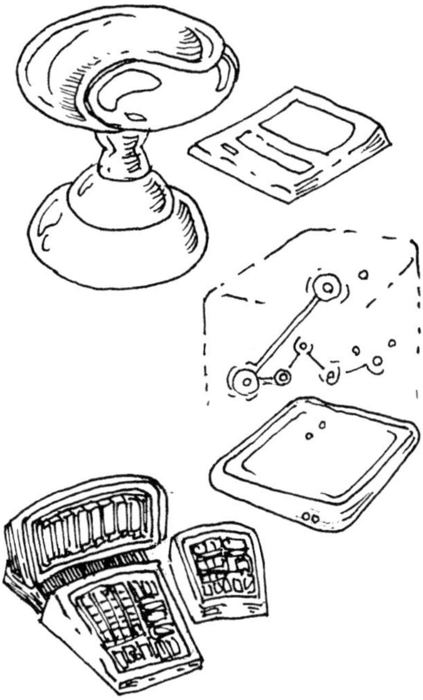

The **computer** does what you would expect; it evaluates data and produces an output based on that data. You can enter data by keyboard, but most computers have scanners so they can scan in a document or photograph and "read" them. For shipboard use, such a computer will have a **projection box**, which is a 3-D screen onto which may be projected potential space routes, as well as giving a print out of the route.

In a **cosmological library**, much data is held electronically and can be accessed at terminals located appropriately. Such are not common; even a magazine as prestigious as *Cosmopolis* has its magazine library as hard copy rather than held electronically.

An **information service** is a more general version of a cosmological library. It will provide basic data on most things.

Included to show the flexibility of the system, the **ledger** can be kept electronically using a keyboard to enter data and displaying the result on a screen. On it can be a book, and the book can be consulted at leisure. Alternatively, the ledger can be a book, but, at convenient intervals, the pages can be read into the ledger and can then be stored electronically to be looked at on the screen.

VEHICLES

Look, there is a universe out there; people walk, ride animals, use rickshaws pulled by indentured labourers, or travel from island to island by dugout canoe. There is an almost infinite variety of vehicles, but I will attempt to give you a quick overview.

Air-cabs are popular on planets with many islands; I remember travelling in such a taxi on Commarice. I failed to be impressed; the metalwork was stained by long exposure to the elements, the glass of the dome was clouded, the pods cratered and corroded. Frankly, I was glad when it landed. Some have an autopilot, some a human operator. Both can be equally ghastly.

Flitters are small flying vehicles; I've known cases where they were small enough to be carried, hidden on a fishing boat. **Float-cars** are somewhat more substantial vehicles; effectively they could be considered flitters with gravitas.

The boundaries between flitters, float-cars, and flyers are blurred. As a rule **flyers** are larger and capable of longer journeys. A flyer can be as small as a two- or four-seater, the passengers protected by a dome of glass (sometimes dark green depending on the local sun). More commonly, they are larger, and the term is often the generic name for a flying bus taking many people or for a local air service.

An example of a small flyer is the **Mitrix flyer**. Used as a trainer, fuel is a charged cell; it has emergency power, navigator, radio, backup box, emergency flares, pistol, emergency water, and emergency gear.*

Transporters are heavy-lift versions of flyers; some can carry considerable quantities of cargo. Some are restricted to working within atmosphere; others are used to take cargo to ships waiting beyond the edge of atmosphere.

* Batteries not included.

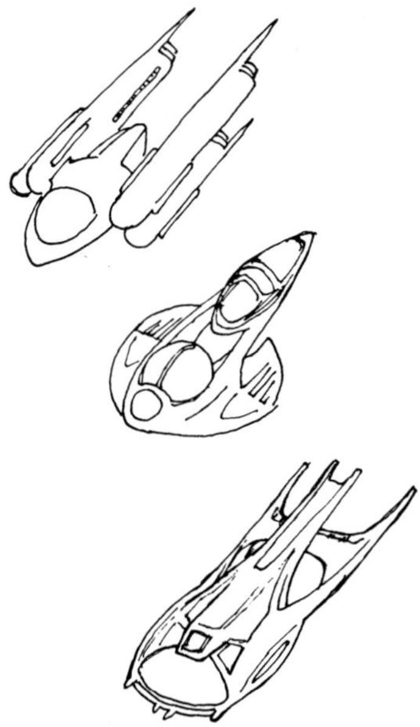

Monorails are common enough to need no introduction; they are found on most industrialised planets.

Power Wagons are used for medium haulage, both along roads and cross country. Found even on planets with good transport infrastructure, as you need something to carry goods to the railhead.

Submarines are still used, mainly for engineering work below the surface of seas and lakes, and in areas where the currents are too strong for divers to work. They are flexible vehicles; one recently advertised for sale second hand had a crew of two, could carry half a dozen passengers and move at fifty knots, and had a range of several thousand miles.

Ah, yes, the comic relief.† **Three-wheeled runabouts** are vehicles produced from all sorts of bits and pieces such as are found on many a score of backwoods worlds.

† Included to prove that not every compiler of such works is a humourless drudge.

WEAPONS

I'm afraid this section was almost left out, but after prolonged editorial agonising it was felt there might be some interest, so we decided to include it anyway.

The **air-tube** is a device for shooting glass needles. The glass needles can merely be that or can carry various chemicals, toxins, aphrodisiacs, or even euphorics.

There is normally an air reservoir to power the device, which can be hand pumped or even blown up like a balloon using the power of the firer's lungs prior to firing.

Daggers are basically knives of a variety of materials; flint is rarely seen much nowadays, but pretty well every metal is used, as well as ceramics and glass. They can be worn on a belt sheath, in a sheath that holds it flat to the haunch, or, in the case of a **throwing blade**, hidden in a sheath on the forearm.

Also known as dart-shooters and dart ejectors, **dart-pistols** are related to the air-tube. Only in this case, the dart is not propelled by air. Normally they are propelled by a small cartridge, but, in some dart ejectors, a strong spring is used.

A specialist version of the dart-pistol, the **dedactor** is a complicated weapon that discharges three sorts of glass needles. The mildest causes a maddening itch of three weeks duration; the others we will not dwell on.

GUNS

These are weapons capable of being fired one handed and are largely short range. They can fire projectiles, which do their damage from kinetic energy (unlike dart-pistols, where the dart is normally just the delivery vehicle for a chemical agent), or they can fire an energy beam. The energy weapons are sometimes called projacs.

A local term used by the happy, laughing people who inhabit Boniface is the **bylo-by**. As in "he carries a bylo-by. Had you touched his ores he would have blown away your head and ears." A gun of sorts.

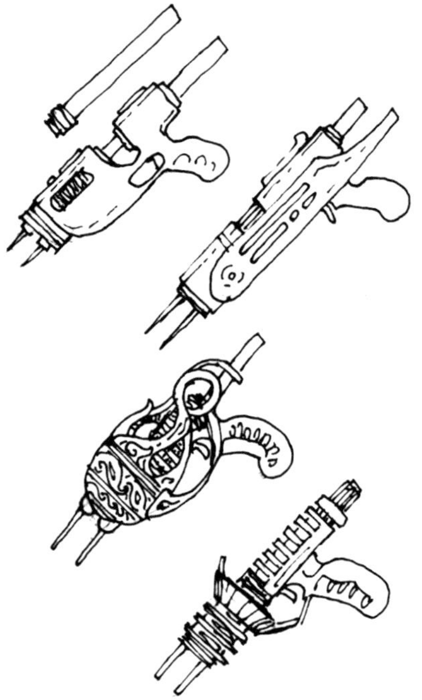

One of the many forms of handgun, the **compact handgun** is, as the name suggests, compact and can be hidden in a lady's sash or even some other more intimate garment. But frankly, they are lacking in firepower; I've known some where you got a bigger shock when you discovered the hiding place than you did from the weapon itself. Compact handguns tend to be projectile; there isn't room for a decent energy cell.

Amongst the energy guns are the **Dys Model G Skull-splitter**, a small weapon easily concealed in the pocket and banned anywhere civilised, and the **Ezelite,** a light gun with a very tight focus, so that it is possible with three shots to punch three entirely separate holes into the back of the victim's head.*

*Why this should be necessary for any reason other than ostentatious display is beyond me. If the victim isn't dead after the first hole, then you're using the wrong weapon. I'd recommend the bylo-by or the Model J projac.

Most energy guns produce "a line of crackling dazzle" rather than a discrete pulse of energy. However, with some models it is possible to change the setting so that the tight focussed beam becomes a broad, and lethal, fan, but with less range. Some examples are the **Model 6a projac,** "popular" because it can be broken down and disguised in the grips and other parts of a travelling bag, and the **Model J projac**, a somewhat more powerful weapon — it will blow the head of a thrombodaxus.

Whilst dealing with guns, it makes sense to look at something a little larger.

A **long gun** is a longer range version of a gun. Bigger, heavier, with a longer barrel, it tends to be used for firing projectiles; there is a general feeling that energy weapons in this category lack authority. Depending on the skill of the user, the range can be out to a mile.

A power-gun is a considerably heavier weapon, normally mounted on a pintle-mount or on a vehicle. It will be capable of rapid fire from a belt or more probably a magazine holding hundreds of rounds. Some can have several barrels that fire simultaneously.

More formally the "Disruptor," the **Ruptor** is a light vehicle-mounted weapon which fires discrete pulses of energy. This it can do because the energy is drawn from the vehicle fuel cells. One pulse will destroy a small shanty.

For those who want even more power, I would recommend the Straidot-Ferox **gunship**;* these are armed with demolition missiles as well as energy weapons of the Ruptor class.

MISCELLANEOUS

Moving away from guns, we have some poison weapons.

A **poison sac** adheres to the first joint of the middle finger, and a needle protrudes from a round gasket on the outer face of the sac. Squeeze the sac, and the contents are injected via the needle. Obviously, you have to stick the needle into someone and then squeeze the sac immediately.

A **poison tube** is a short glass tube four inches long; it comes pre-loaded with an appropriate powder. To use, point the tube at the target's face and blow the other end.†

We then have body weapons, built into the person and not obvious to the casual observer. These tend to be found in certain specialist communities, and we give only a couple of examples.

To turn a **finger** into a hidden weapon, operate on it and replace the bone. When activated, a thin mist comes from the pointed finger; the mist will be a gas of choice but ideally is not corrosive.

The **optical laser** is another specialist weapon; small lasers are surgically attached to the optical muscles so that a laser beam can be directed down line of sight. The beam is modulated as necessary to produce maximum hypnotic potency. When the beam strikes the victim's retina, the signal induces hypnotic coma.

We then have the weapons of the true eccentrics.

The **flame staff** is created by installing a tubular device to the end of any staff. One merely has to touch the trigger, and the tube spouts a long flame. Basically, it is a one-shot weapon.

The **iron-toed slipper** is a weapon of desperation if there ever was one. Unless used by an expert, the iron toe will do more damage to the wearer than to the victim. They are therefore often worn over firmer footwear.

I could go on, but frankly I refused point blank to cover flashaways, pinkers, and spantics. There are things even a hack will not do for money!

* Irritatingly known as gunboats by some pedantic commentators.

† Do not, under any circumstances, inhale.